Footprints in a
Small Town

All the Best !!

DAVID MICHAEL LEE

David Michael Lee

Footprint Publications

ISBN-10: 198692002X
ISBN-13: 978-1986920025

DEDICATION

Dedicated to my wife, Pamela, my children, Crystal, Nathan, Adam, Cassidy and my grandchildren Indiana and Brody

Special dedication to my mother, Agnes E. Lee

In Memory of Robert "Bobby" Lee, Larry Mills, Harold "Buster" Chandler and Bryan Blakely

I want to have pride like my mother has,
And not like the kind in the Bible that turns you bad.
And I want to have friends that I can trust,
that love me for the man I've become and not the man that I was.

"The Perfect Space" by The Avett Brothers

TABLE OF CONTENTS

ACKNOWLEDGMENTS

Special Appreciation to my wife Pamela. Thank you for your love, patience and understanding when I started this endeavor. You will forever be "home" to me. I want to thank Denise Williams, Laurie Haar and Lynn Michelle Salyer for their assistance in the edit process and for their words of encouragement. I also want to thank the faithful and dedicated readers of my blog, "Footprints of a Legacy Left Behind". In addition, I want to recognize the Blakely family for making me feel like one of their own. I want to acknowledge Bob Emrich, Steve Schueren and Bryan Blakely for their friendship and influence in my life… rest in peace my brothers, I will carry on until we meet again. In closing, I want to give honor and praise to my Savior, Jesus Christ. Thank you for your grace and the way of Salvation you have provided for this world.

NOTE: Not one word of this book was written without music intentionally streaming in the background. Acknowledgment is given to the music of MercyMe, Dan Folgelberg, Glenn Campbell, Dwight Yoakham, Jack's Mannequin, The Martin's, Casting Crown's, The Temptations, Sanctus Real, Trisha Yearwood, Tom Petty, The Undeserving, Keith Green, Patsy Cline, David Phelps, Frank Turner, Clay Kirchenbauer, ELO, The Avett Brothers, Bob Seger, Mae, Cassidy Guzman, James Taylor, Collective Soul, The Beatles, Joe Walsh and The Sidewalk Prophets.

INTRODUCTION

I am often asked where I am from. Almost always, the question is simply a kind gesture from a new acquaintance. It is common, and it is meant to start a conversation. The reality is no one is really that interested in your answer, but it is protocol to levitate the strange awkwardness of meeting someone you don't know.

Most times my response is met with a blank stare that indicates they have no idea where Oak Harbor, Ohio, is located. Other times, it elicits a slight shake of the head and a tactful response to the possibility that they may have once passed through it on a road trip a long time ago.

When I was younger, when asked, I would answer enthusiastically and always with pride. I would do my best to give a clear picture of where my hometown was. Then, as I got older, I noticed that nearly every time I told people where I was from I delivered, "Oak Harbor," as if it was the punchline to a bad joke. There would be silence and I would wait for that familiar blank stare. I would then say… "Oak Harbor is in Northwest, Ohio, just off Lake Erie… close to Cedar Point" and suddenly I would see their eyes light up with recognition.

I guess referencing the fact that my hometown is near Cedar Point is enough for some people to acknowledge its existence. But for those of us that were raised there, we know that this town is so much more than just being "close" to Cedar Point.

My hope is that as you read this book, you will come away with a deeper appreciation of another place and time in your life. Maybe your thoughts will stir, and you will once again experience the memories of your youth. With any luck, you may even remember an old friendship and perhaps a story or two that you may have forgotten.

Hopefully, you'll be able to find the footprints that you made in your small town all those years ago.

David Michael Lee

David Michael Lee

1

FOOTPRINTS

I haven't "lived" in Oak Harbor for many years, it is just a place where I drive through every now and then. Most times to reminisce of the past, but sometimes to find something "new" and see what has changed. While many things have changed over the years, there are some things that have been the same way for as long as I can remember.

I must admit, it is an odd experience to drive through this small town that has existed only in your memory for almost 40 years. When I drive through, I feel a bit like a ghost everywhere I go. I was a resident of this small town from another time, yet as I search for what is the same and what has changed, I am moving through someone else's present day. It is a strange experience because I have clear memories of being a part of it and of what it was, and the people I see do not know that it was part of me. They have no recollection of who I am, and their memories of this same small town are different than mine.

It's funny that the everyday places & events where we lived our lives are often the most elusive to find in our photo albums. We often have snapshots of holidays, graduations, and other special events, but the neighborhood, the school we went to every day, or the park we played in are rarely captured on film. They are just images that flash across our memory that fade over time.

These memories find their way to me when I find myself back in a familiar environment; the place I played my first baseball game, the store I used to buy candy, the school room of my favorite teacher, or the house I celebrated the 'best Christmas ever' as a kid. None of these childhood memories are that remarkable to anyone else but they mean an INCREDIBLE amount to me. Many of these emotions I feel are very personal and come gushing out from the hidden corners of my heart.

When I was living in Oak Harbor, people came and went all the time and it never seemed like a big deal. But, as soon as I went away to college, I began to view the place of my upbringing much differently. Perhaps it was simply a case of nostalgia, but each time I returned home to the place where I found my feet I could not help but take pleasure in summoning to mind the ghosts of my past and the memories. I would come home and look to see if the footprints I placed around town were still there.

While I was convinced I would one day replace those memories and footprints with shinier ones. I now realize that I was too eager to replace the memories of my childhood. I made the mistake that generations of young adults have done since the beginning of time. I wanted to grow up and move on with life faster than what needed to be. The memories of growing up in Oak Harbor during that time would forever be mine and mine alone to preserve and to share.

Whenever anyone moved away, only one or two people ever really kept in touch with those that left. I was no different. It wasn't long after I left that my friends, the same friends who I thought meant everything to me, had moved on. That just confirmed to me that it was hard on those of us that left the safe confines of our hometown. The faster you accepted the fact that you were now just someone they used to know, the better it was for you.

As important as I may have thought myself to be, life in Oak Harbor went on well without my presence and apart from a few of the good memories held in the minds of my closest friends, it's as if I had never lived there.

For so long I felt guilty about not keeping strong ties with the place that had nurtured me. When things in your life change, it's impossible to hold on to what you had and impossible to make things go back to the way they used to be. I wasn't aware that time would erase the vivid clarity of the footprints and memories I placed there so long ago. I wish so clearly that I could go back and re-experience some of them once more.

In many ways, that is the reason for this book. It is for me to remember and relive the events I had experienced so long ago. I want it to clarify to my family why I am the way that I am. I cannot deny the influence this town had on my upbringing, and in many ways, it shaped and molded me into who I would become.

I would love to tell all these stories with nostalgic, feel good "happy-endings" but not all my stories are like that. Some are filled with disappointment and hurt. However, there are a few that are filled with joy and happiness that have given me hope in knowing that there are truly wonderful aspects of growing up in small-town America.

Ultimately, this story is intended for my family, more importantly my children and grandchildren. I write this so that they will know where I came from and, in a small way, have a piece of me that will endure long after I am gone. I want to be remembered and I want future generations of my family to know that I existed. I realize that sounds and feels so self- promoting and arrogant when I write those words down, but what is the purpose of life and living if you don't leave a legacy that is to be remembered? Hopefully, you anticipate your legacy will be remembered, maybe even in a good way, but there are no guarantees.

Truth is, if you are not remembered in the eyes of the local community you grew up in, your "hometown," the chances of your passing being noticed are slim. One day I am going to die and outside of my family it will probably get little notice. Maybe someone will be sad or write a nice note on my wife's Facebook page. My obituary will be posted in the local paper and after a few days people will move on. I'm not whining, it's just the cycle of life and it will happen to you too. However, if your life is reminisced by those who love you likely you will be remembered forever.

My intention is to give those who read these stories a glimpse of what it was like for me to grow up in small-town America in the 1960's and 1970's. It is intended to be as frank and personal as I can possibly make it. I will not intentionally censor myself and I will try to keep it as factual as possible. I will tell the truth as I had experienced it or, at the very least, how I perceived it. I have tried not to stray from the spirit and the sequence of events as they happened.

There is no doubt that I have lost some clarity of the footprints and memories I made over those years. There are details that I used to be able to easily recollect, even as recent as a few years ago, but I can't anymore. I am not alarmed too much about my memory loss. I am pretty sure I am not suffering from any medical problem leading to unusual memory loss. I believe it is just a natural process of life that is being orchestrated by something… that something is TIME.

Time marches on, like a faceless army – emotionless, merciless, relentless and all-consuming. Time creeps slowly but surely pillaging the precious memories of our past. People say, "time heals" but what they really mean is that "time erodes." Time erodes everything – the bad, the ugly, and even the good. Time erodes the details so that sometimes memories cross and blur into one another. I look at some of the things I used to do when Oak Harbor was home and I want to re-connect with my past. However, I don't live there anymore. I am forced to rely on the memories that fill my mind.

I admit that I have thought about the fact that maybe time isn't the real enemy. Possibly, the real enemy is the attachment to memories that I am not sure ever existed the way I remember them. Over the years, I have told myself that this is silly. Why am I trying to re-connect to a place that doesn't even remember that I was part of it?

It is then I am reminded of the many nights I lie awake with memories of another place and time running through my thoughts. I long to find the footprints of my past and I cannot deny the fact that there is something deep inside of me that is pushing me to find my way back home. Even if that home isn't what I thought it to be.

The closest I can come to explaining how I wrote the book you are holding in your hands is to say that it was like restoring a cracked and faded photograph. The picture of the 60s and 70s was hard to focus on. There was so much change and it truly was a unique time in America. Most people think of the stereotypes such as radical changes in musical tastes, the revolution of sexual attitudes, urban race riots, assassinations, Kent State, Watergate, athletes taken hostage and murdered at the Olympics and who can forget the pain of Vietnam.

It was even more difficult when you consider the location of my stories. Everything that takes place in these stories happens in Oak Harbor, Ohio. There was a foot still firmly planted in the 50s and change had yet to cross the boundaries of our small-town. Like most other things that happened in Oak Harbor, change took place so slowly and so gradually that we hardly noticed it at all.

I carry memories of innocence, happiness, joy and at times pain, hurt and loss. They have made me who I am. I have re-traced the footprints that I could find, and I have put them into words. My greatest hope is that, in reading this book, you may be reminded of the special times in your life too, even if some of them were difficult.

I know that all of us have stories from our youth.

These footprints and stories are mine.

2

GROWING UP HARTFORD

Oak Harbor is a small Ohio village located 10 miles inland from the mouth of the Portage River.

From the very beginning in 1832, when Joseph Wardlow laid down the boundaries of a settlement that would be incorporated in 1835 as the Village of Hartford, this place was settled for the benefit of the family. Starting with two or three cabins in the wilderness, people were willing to take a risk and pursue their dream of a community that would flourish.

Then in 1838, Adolphus Kraemer, an industrious man who dreamed of establishing a prosperous town, bought the land of the Hartford area. By 1850, this fledgling community became a village of thirty-eight dwellings with one hundred eighty-seven people.

It had plotted streets, two churches, a school, a thriving lumber industry, farming and some manufacturing businesses. It was growing fast and people were drawn to the opportunities that were available in this new town.

The small village of Hartford was a haven for families trying to raise their children in an environment that would produce wholesome and hardworking future families. Most of the people that grew up there would never stray far from this place. The townspeople took pride in the fact that they would not be willing to

6

drift far from the goals and principles that were established when the town was founded.

The citizens of Hartford soon discovered that they had a problem. With the growth of the village, it became necessary to establish a post office. Because there were three other villages with the name "Hartford" in Ohio, the Post Office requested a name change.

In 1863, the village of Hartford officially became the Village of Oak Harbor. It was named "Oak" to emphasize the prominence of that wood in the surrounding area, and "Harbor" for the importance of the river to the village. The name changed but not the goal and principles that were established when it was incorporated under the name of Hartford.

Over the course of the next 100 years, Oak Harbor continued to re-invent itself and grow with the times. Then it seems as if the fledgling town seemed to hit a wall and once you got past the well-maintained streets and neatly manicured lawns, Oak Harbor seemed to be about a decade off from the rest of the world. When other communities were expanding and bringing in new technologies, Oak Harbor was struggling to embrace an ever-changing world. There seemed to be a desperate attempt at keeping the outside world from entering our community. They simply were not interested in change.

So, in the 1960's, Oak Harbor was solidly set in the early 1950's. In reflection, I am sure it was indeed somewhat romantic and ideal from the outside looking in. I could see why my parents looked at Oak Harbor as a wonderful place to raise their children and protect them from the things in the world.

This is where I grew up.

Yes, the name was Oak Harbor, but the values and principles upon which we were raised can clearly be traced back to the days when this town was known as Hartford.

What does growing up Hartford mean?

Personally, it meant growing up in a place where kids didn't think twice about playing on someone else's lawn or riding your bikes with abandon throughout the town. Where we could still go for a walk at dusk without fear of your picture ending up on a billboard at the local post office or on the side of a milk carton. It's where everyone knew everyone else.

Our summer days were filled with swimming at Teagarden's (the community pool), baseball games and 4th of July celebrations at Veteran's Park, hanging out with your friends at the dairy queen and the fair. The cold, snow-filled days of winter, were filled with sledding, skating at Gleckler's pond, watching the Rocket's play on the stage basketball court and the occasional neighborhood snowball fight. Not to mention the cheeseburger and fries you'd get at Van Atta's Restaurant for $1.25 while sitting at your table reading one of the magazines from the rack like it was your own personal library. I still cannot believe they let us do that.

As a child, and even into my teen years, I knew my hometown intimately, and it knew me. It seemed that no matter where I went, I would always run into something that reminded me of how much I'd already done there. Every day it would wrap around me like a warm blanket on a cold winter's night until I felt I knew it as intimately as I did the layout of my own bedroom. I could walk around it with my eyes closed and never be surprised by a single thing.

Everything outside the boundaries of my hometown was kind of a blur. I could only imagine what everyday life was like in faraway cities. Those places outside of the town limit signs could be just as much a figment of my imagination as anything else I've ever dreamed. No matter how many pictures I saw, or how many times people would come back with stories of life beyond your reality, it just never seemed too convincing. To me, those places were as much a fantasy and as far away as the land of Oz.

Yet, somewhere along the way, I made an impassioned decision that I "had to get out," and I made plans to leave. Why did I make this decision? I only can say that I wondered what was out there. I needed to know what was found beyond the confines of the town limits.

Everything I did focused on breaking free from Oak Harbor and starting again somewhere else. It was as though every aspect of my life and who I was as a person would change immediately upon changing zip codes. I can remember the strange sense of pity for those around me who weren't leaving. I imagine some of my friends wanted to stay. Others, I felt at the time, were permanently trapped in the quagmire of familiarity and convenience. They never had the opportunity to leave.

I think there is a feeling of excitement when you are escaping from something. But there is always fear. Fear of the unknown and the fear of leaving a place that was home. However, by leaving, you discover that there are so many things you don't know about yourself and stepping outside your comfort zone in such a profound way helps you peel back those layers of who you really are. One layer at a time.

Leaving and moving away from Oak Harbor allowed me to grow. It gave me the opportunity to change and to have some influence on what I wanted to do with my life. However, there will always be a part of me that will remain the same. I am someone that remembers my roots and where I came from. Those roots... the roots of Hartford, were instilled in me at an early age and I remember them.

As the date of leaving Oak Harbor and heading off to college was inching ever closer, I began to realize just how much of me was part of this small town. I would miss the people, I would miss the familiar streets I walked over and over. I never had a fear of something bad happening to me when I would walk around. There is a peaceful comfort in knowing one's surroundings intimately, a certainty that lends confidence to whoever experiences it. It's hard not to feel like the master of your domain when there is not a single nook of your territory you haven't explored. I had to ask myself who would I be without such comfort? Who would I become when everything was foreign? What would happen when I was the visitor of a new town I wanted to make my home?

The day I left was amongst the most bittersweet of my life. I hid the embarrassing tears as best I could in front of my mom. I made plans to call and promised to come back as much as possible and walk these same streets. I promised myself, above all, not to forget the memories. I would convince myself that I would never grow so cold or so different that I couldn't come back and fit the puzzle piece where I left it when I first went away.

But it isn't that easy. You're leaving and though you'll come back and visit, the moments you had there will never be recreated. The many summer nights that unfolded in unassuming ease — the long car rides with friends around the loop, the impromptu parties in a friend's backyard, the conversations that lasted until the wee hours of the morning. These will all soon be vague memories of a different era.

I would return, but it would never be the same. Returning to my hometown would have a quality of nostalgia to it that prevented me from fully embracing the moment. Sure, I would see old friends, but my time would be limited as to prevent much outside of reminiscing about the times we created.

When I would come back to visit, I began to see people and things differently. When you see them through the eyes of a visitor, there is so much you don't understand or relate to anymore. You have grown up, changed shape, and you no longer fit back into that puzzle piece.

It is then you realize that the house where you grew up, isn't home anymore. You are faced with coming to terms with the fact that everything has changed and you know you will never get that back. You get the overwhelming feeling of being a visitor and you feel homesick for a place that doesn't even exist anymore.

I am reminded that there was a person that existed before I left, that is entirely contained in and defined by where I grew up. For me, going back to visit is like trying to grab a handful of air in a burst of wind — I am surrounded by who I once was, but I am never able to completely re-connect to it. Things changed, and I would have to learn to accept that.

Maybe it's a rite of passage of life. I am not sure. I chose to leave, and I would never again feel at home in the town I grew up in. I would soon realize, to sense the same feeling of home, I would eventually have to create a new home for me, my kids and for my family. As hard as I tried to do that, I could never replace the same feelings I had when I was growing up in Oak Harbor.

Those of us that experienced it, know that there was something special about growing up there.

Again… it wasn't perfect. There has always been a down side to living in a small town.

However, there will always be evidence of the goodness and

wholesome, hometown pride that was apparent when the village of Hartford was founded. It is still there. You don't have to look too hard for it. I believe it is ingrained and part of anyone who grew up there.

I know for me, it is part of who I am, and I will forever be grateful for growing up "Hartford".

3

FINDING THE WORDS

I struggle to know exactly how to begin. There really isn't enough space to tell everything and I don't want to tell too much. My fear is that I will bore you with insignificant or uninteresting details of my life, but I guess I need to start with some background so that you can understand where I am coming from.

For anyone who knows me, it is no secret that I have loved to write from the moment I learned to put sentences together in Mrs. Milbrodt's second-grade class at R.C. Waters Elementary School.

There is a big reason for this.

For as long as I remember I have been embarrassed if I have to speak in front of a group of people. One-on-one I was fine, but get me in front of people I would immediately have issues. I would struggle and mix my words up and say them out of order. That was one of the primary reasons why I focused on writing and not talking. I have spent most of life trying to hide this from people. It has been such a guarded secret that, even now, I struggle with sharing it with you. There have been periods of my life when it has been more evident than other times. It is something that I have had to deal with my whole life. I don't talk about it much because it is something that I have had to work very hard at not doing. I have learned to mask it even from my own family.

I must avoid certain situations to keep myself from doing it. Unless you experience it or have the problem yourself, you cannot fully understand the gravity and challenge it is to have what I have to deal with. I only reveal it now because it is something that is key as to why I react to certain things that happen in my life.

I am a stutterer.

To be more exact, I suffer from what is called "involuntary hesitation" which basically means I hesitate in my speech. I hesitate so that I don't stumble over my words. I cannot control it and the more I try to stop "hesitating" the worse it gets. It causes me to talk fast and loud in order to get my words out of my mouth.

It doesn't sound too bad or serious when you just write the words down. However, the experience of having the problem is much worse than I ever could have imagined. I must always be on guard to make sure I control it when it happens. However, there is a time when I have absolutely no problem responding or showing any signs of hesitation in my speech. I have no symptoms when I am angry. I have clarity of speech; clarity of thought and I do not stumble over one single word. Like Mel Tillis, who doesn't stutter when he sings, I do not stutter when I am angry.

It is something that has been a lifelong problem for me. My frustration at putting my words together sometimes results in having a sharp tongue and a short temper. It doesn't ever excuse my improper response, but it is an underlying problem that I must deal with every day.

To cope, I learned how to write and put sentences together all those years ago in Mrs. Milbrodt's class. I found so much comfort in putting my feelings and memories down on paper. I wrote all the way through my high school and college years.

After I graduated from college, I received a gift from a close friend of mine. I slowly opened the gift box and pulled out a beautiful Waterford pen. It felt great in my hand and immediately I knew that it was meant to tell stories. It was meant to share thoughts, beliefs, feelings, and perspectives. It was meant to be used. All it and I needed was a blank piece of paper.

I continued to write. I wrote about everything. I wrote about growing up in Oak Harbor and my family. I wrote about losing loved ones. I wrote about my elementary, junior high and high school experiences. I wrote about college. I wrote about traveling around the world, meeting two U.S. Presidents and I re-told stories that my grandfather shared with me. I wrote about my future dreams and how I truly felt about the things in my life. I wrote every day and I kept my reflections in notebooks and hid them so that no one would ever find them. I was embarrassed, afraid that someone would find them and expose my thoughts and feelings. It was my life story, hand-written and detailed on paper. I hid it from everybody, including my own family. Nobody ever knew that this was what I did in my spare time. It was a long time ago. Long before there were computers in every home. Long before word processors and the internet existed.

But like things always do, life got in my way. Responsibilities of a young father and a man trying to save his marriage and make it in this life sapped any desire and passion I had for writing. It appeared to me, that a dark cloud covered my memories and I just could not bring myself to fight my way through it.

I just simply stopped writing and put the pen down.

Everything I had written about over those years will never be read by anyone. Somewhere around the age of 25, I permanently hid those notebooks and today they are where I placed them all those years ago. I am sure that my "best" writings are embedded somewhere in those notebooks. I have no ability to unearth them. Along with my treasured Waterford Pen, those notebooks will remain where I put them all those years ago.

For the next 20 years, I really did not write much more than my sign my name. I swallowed the desire and passion I had for writing. I did everything I could to keep those feelings in check and buried in my past.

Then something changed. I started to wake up in the middle of the night with stories flooding my thoughts. I couldn't sleep, and I had the uncontrollable urge to put these thoughts down. There it was, my passion I had for writing had finally found its way through the darkness.

I got up out of bed and turned on my computer. I did some

research and quickly downloaded a blog program. I did not have a clue as to what a "blog" was. While I have always loved to write, this blogging thing was different. This was where people would be able to actually read what you wrote. I'd never blogged before. I never really had anyone read my stories and I didn't even know how people would find my website, or if they'd even like it. I looked at some other blogs and I was amazed at how many people wrote and posted every day. I knew I couldn't post every day because I was sure that I would run out of things to say.

Facing that empty computer screen for the first time, I must admit, I was scared. I was doubtful. Something inside me told me that if I didn't write right then, these stories would begin to fade again. I did not want to face another day where I did not put these stories down. I knew if I didn't start right then it would lead to another wasted day, which would become another wasted month – and another wasted year of my life. I did not want that... so I started to write. Now, I realize I didn't just say I performed my first brain surgery, or I decided to run for president. But for me, it was a pivotal day – one that will shape the rest of my life.

So, I wrote, and I was soon publishing articles and stories. I always say that "I love to write, but that doesn't mean that I am a good writer." Some of my posts are not bad and a few of them I would have to admit are pretty good. Many of them are just "ok" and a portion of them are simply not good.

If you've read my writings, you know that I love sharing personal stories. I have never been able to write stories about someone else, so I usually write about myself. That isn't as self-serving as that may come across. It is just that I share my thoughts and things that I know about. I know about failure and I know about success. I have experienced both at extreme levels.

Since that night when I downloaded that blog program, there have not been many days where I did not write something. Some of those stories and posts have made their way onto my blog site. However, many articles and stories will forever remain drafts, never to be published. Not because they are not good stories, but rather because I am not at peace about revealing them for people to read. I am sure that on some levels, they contain my "best" writing. I have yet to fully understand why I choose to write some of the stories I do. What

I do know is that there is a stirring inside of me, something telling me that tomorrow isn't supposed to look like yesterday. I have a compulsion to document my stories and put them down so that they don't fade away over time.

After a few years of writing, I realized that I had something that money could not buy: time preserved. Once again, I had some of the stories of my life growing up in Oak Harbor down on paper and I had no idea what to do with them this time. I had written all these same stories before when I was younger, but I buried them years ago and now I wanted to ensure that I could preserve them. I wanted to safeguard them so that they would be documented before I would forget them or lose them when my computer failed. I made up my mind that I was going to collect these stories and put them in a book for my family.

Most people look back at their teenage years and have pleasant memories of nostalgia. I don't have that luxury. Yes, the great times were there, in generous quantity, but they were mixed with heartache and hurt. One set of emotions, quickly replaced by another. Sometimes within hours of each other. I experienced these old feelings and emotions again when I started writing these stories down.

Writing is not for the faint of heart. Writing is hard. It takes an emotional toll on your heart. You pour yourself into it and sometimes, after people read them, they are not so kind and stomp on your heart or your perspective. I have had some great supporters of my writings and I have had some detractors. I have been called names and I have had someone call my writings, "A stain on the white shirt of society." I have come close to quitting many times over the years, but I still cannot walk away from it.

Through writing, I've got to know some amazing people I'd never have had reason or opportunity to know otherwise. Many of them have grown to be genuine friends – some of them an ocean away. Some readers even credit my posts with giving them the nudge they needed to launch out into their own deep waters, which is the highest compliment to me.

But most of all – best of all – writing allowed me to feel more like "me" than I had in years.

However, being "me" doesn't lessen the fear of having people read your stories. I struggle with questions like, "What if no one likes my stories?" "What if someone leaves me a really mean comment?" "What if I'm criticized?" "What if my stories are only interesting to me?" "What if this book is a mistake?"

Those are just a few of the questions that I fear.

At no point in my life did the thought of writing a book ever cross my mind, until a few days before I started to write it. As weird as it sounds, it felt like this was something I had to do. And I'll be honest, most of my life has been like that – where suddenly, I feel compelled to do something I've never even thought about before.

In addition, early on in writing these stories, I was so worried about every sentence, every word, every comma, every semi-colon and every little detail of each chapter. It ate away at me. I was caught up in writing three sentences and then stop and delete two and a half of them. I felt like it had to be perfect, so no one would criticize me.

I tried to convince myself to just ignore this huge weight inside of me, but I couldn't do it. So, I talked myself into writing about the real things that happened to me. I had to share from my heart and from my perspective. That's when I stopped caring about every single word, sentence, comma, semi-colon, and detail. That's when I learned how to write from my heart.

There are so many rules about how to write and what to write about. I try not to follow any of them – it's just not me. I never know what I'm going to say when I sit down and write. I also don't know when the words are going to come out. I just sit down with a topic and maybe one line that I wrote down on my notepad and go from there. I can't plan ahead, and I write until I'm satisfied.

I'm not here just to write random words. Everything must mean something. I am not trying to just put words down on paper and I surely not aiming for apathy from the reader. If you're going to read my writing, I'm going to do my best to make sure you walk away with something from it. Something that will make you think and maybe something that will move your heart.

Writing has given me so much and has taught me even more. It's made me realize how powerful our words really are. I can say anything I want. Much like when I speak, all I must do is put the words in the right order. I just need to find the words. When I do that, I get a satisfaction that I cannot explain. Stories and perspectives just flow out and it calms me. The weight on my mind and heart is lifted.

4

NO SILVER SPOONS

Maya Angelou once said that "The ache for home lives in all of us." It's a universal truth. Studies have shown that one-third of American adults over the age of 30 had revisited their childhood homes (houses they lived in from ages 5 to 12). The journey was made usually for one of three reasons: a desire to reconnect with childhood, a need to reflect on a past crisis, or the hope for closure resulting from unfinished business. For me, I think all three of those reasons are why I am writing this book.

It makes sense to go back to my Walnut Street home. I left my innocence there, somewhere between dimly lit ceilings and the hardwood floors. Every now and then, I will make my way to Walnut Street to drive past the house that I consider my "home." The other houses I have lived in were just that... houses. Houses do not make a home.

Every now and then I will drive past my home. I fool myself into thinking that one day when I drive past, maybe just maybe, it would be just like I always pictured it in my thoughts. The familiar screen door would be there, and I would be able to envision my mom standing there, holding it open for me when I came home from school. I would be able to walk into the kitchen and smell the dinner that she had made for us.

From memory, I can walk each step of the house. I remember

every nook and cranny. Every detail, right down to the linoleum floor that made up the bathroom floor.

Unfortunately, reality begs to differ. Reality is that the house is smaller than I remember it — the colors, rough and faded; the screen door, gone. The staggered three-window front door is still the same after all these years, thankfully, but the door is weathered and has paid a price for being exposed to the elements. Some of the windows have been replaced and the garage has seen better years. Trees have been cut down and the well-worn path through our backyard to Blakely's house has disappeared long ago.

One day, a few years back, I had the nerve to stop and walk up to the side door and knock. I wasn't sure what I was going to say if someone answered the door. I looked through the window next to the door and from what I could see, it looked just like I remembered it. No one came to the door and I haven't had the nerve to stop again.

I don't drive past the house as often anymore. After you see nothing but a pale, strange, shadow of your past so many times, you start to lose the nostalgia of it. Reality starts to replace the memories of the past. I can't allow these new images to kill all my childhood memories. I don't need to find out that the house is more rundown than I remembered. I don't need to know that the line of grape vines that lined my path through the backyard is gone. I don't need to see the tree planted in the backyard by my brother is now cut down. I don't want anything to replace the memories of our Walnut Street home, even if some of those memories are horrific.

My experience isn't unique. While visiting our childhood home is cathartic for the majority of those who make the trip, many who visit their childhood home experience a shattering of expectations, upset that their beloved house has changed, or they realize that they cannot return to that place of childhood happiness. I constantly find myself going through those same feelings of disillusionment.

I'm not sure what I expect to find when I make these trips back to the old neighborhood; I guess I am trying to reconnect with my childhood and the hope for closure resulting from my experiences from that period.

It's not easy to travel back in time.

I have asked other people about their earliest memory and most of the time people can't give a clear answer. For me, my earliest memory that I remember is a scary clown face that made up the light switch on the wall of my bedroom on Benton Street in Oak Harbor. I have no other real memory of that house. Most of my childhood memories are centered around the house we moved into on Walnut Street, on New Year's Day in 1964.

My family is made up of my father, Robert, my mother, Agnes and my brothers James (Jim) and Robert (Bobby) and my sister Linda. In addition to our core family, our cousin Larry Mills lived with us for a few years.

My father was a truck driver and my mother a homemaker.

I am the youngest of the children and have always been treated accordingly. I was born into a family that on the outside looked moderately "traditional" in the way of the early 1960's. Dad worked. Mom raised the kids.

The inside of our Walnut Street home was influenced by the love and care from my mother. Simply put, my mother found her happiness in her children. She was the constant foundation in our lives. She loved us unconditionally and ultimately lived her life through our lives. Within our family tree, we range the full spectrum of types, from the flamboyant to the demure, from the repellent to the ideal. My mother set the standard of the "ideal" in my family tree.

She is the most capable person I have ever known. Had she decided to do something different with her life, I have no doubt that she would have been successful in anything she determined to do. She chose to be a wife to my dad and a mom to my brothers, my sister and me. She was a woman of an era where the standard choice was to stay at home and raise the children. She did that with love and great wisdom.

Agnes Elizabeth Clemens was born in November of 1931 in Washington, Pennsylvania. She was the oldest of eight children born to William and Lida (Baker) Clemens. Her young life was filled with events and situations that would have defeated and broken the spirit of most of the young girls her age. Times were hard, and things were tough. That's not to say there were not good times, but as I remember my mother telling me stories of her childhood, there always seemed to be a common theme... nothing stayed "good" for long. She felt as if she had the responsibility of her family on her shoulders, with no real help in sight. She was forced to grow up way too soon. She left home at 17 and left Pennsylvania and never looked back. She had to make decisions that would affect her for the rest of her life. Had not it been for that Greyhound Bus breaking down outside Sandusky, Ohio, God only knows what would have happened to her.

She put her childhood and her past on the shelf, eventually met and married my Dad, became a mother and looked to the future. Her dreams and desires for her life were now solely surrounded in her children. I have never known her to do one thing in this life where she did not put her children first. She sacrificed her own possibilities for the chance that her children could have, do and become more than she ever had the chance to do. She hurt when we hurt. She hoped when we couldn't find hope. She dreamed bigger dreams for us than we've ever dreamed for ourselves. She convinced us that we were worthy of it all... because we were special... to her, we always had been. Her love is beautifully irrational. She looked beyond our faults and flaws and saw the very best version of each of us.

Truly, a mother's love and influence are among the most powerful things a person could ever find in this world. If you doubt it, compare notes with someone who no longer has their mom – or someone who never had her to begin with. For better or worse, no one shapes our lives more than our mother because they do it from the inside out. We find their fingerprints on everything – from our grandest deeds to our most tucked away inner-thoughts.

Ma, Mom, Mommy. She took this role very seriously and never wavered. No matter what. And she was always there for me – and for my brothers and my sister (and for many others). Always.

I have said it before and I will say it to my dying breath... any good quality that I show in my life is directly given to me by my mother.

Hemingway once wrote: "The world breaks everyone, and afterward many are strong at the broken places." My mother was one of those people who healed stronger in the broken places. Despite great obstacles, she bounced back repeatedly from an extremely difficult childhood and choices she shouldn't have had to make at such a young age. My mom is the strongest person I have ever known, and she will always be the one-true North for our family.

My father was born four months before the Wall Street Crash of 1929. Robert James Lee came into this world just as the world stopped partying in the Roaring 20's. My dad was the oldest child born to James and Mildred (Heisey) Lee. I don't really know much about my father's childhood. I have brought it up a few times, but it never really produces a clear picture of his younger years.

What I do know is that at the young age of 16, he enlisted in the Navy. Off he went and when he came back he took a job at Philco in Sandusky, Ohio, where he met my mother.

Shortly after they were married they took off for San Diego because he re-enlisted into the Navy. After his second stint in the Navy ended they made their way back to Ohio with a baby in tow. My brother Jim was born while they were stationed in California. He took a job with Norwalk Truckline and started a long career as a truck driver.

In the coming years, our family would grow with the addition of my brother Bobby, my sister Linda and me.

My dad was an absent father. Not necessarily always by his own choice, but by a career that he chose. Maybe I should say it chose him. Either way, he wasn't there. As children, we did not know him in the way that one can know their father. We did not know what he was like as a child or even what his true dreams and desires were for his life.

As I noted, my father was a truck driver. A true truck driver is a unique breed. There are very few true truck drivers left anymore. My dad was a great truck driver. He drove for over 40 years and never had an accident. Truck drivers may be legally married to another person; however; ultimately they are physically, emotionally and even spiritually married to the road. My father was someone who showed up on weekends. He never made it to the ball games or the plays. In my entire life, I have absolutely no recollection of him being at one of the activities or games I was a part of.

He would come in late on Friday and leave on Sunday afternoon. The short periods he would come home influenced what we did learn about him. All too often these times at home were punctuated by the frustration of children that did not know their father and a man that did not know his own children.

I don't think my father and I looked each other in the eye to tell each other we loved each other until he was well into his sixties. I must say that my dad did what most fathers did from that generation. I know my father loved us. He just showed it differently than how I showed my love for my children. He showed it by going to work and working hard to provide for his family. If you would ask him if he loved his children, he would respond by saying, "Of course I do… I went to work for them every day."

One of the greatest traits that he passed on to each of his children was a good work ethic. My dad answered the bell every time work called. I owe much gratitude to my father for showing each of us the honor that comes from being a good employee and a hard worker.

My brother Jim was the first born. He is nine years older than me and by the time I was old enough to get to know him as someone besides simply being my brother he was gone. He grew up fast and he married his high school sweetheart shortly after high school.

I have to say that Jim was there in my early years, he was my little league baseball coach and he showed up to almost all the athletic events that I was involved in throughout junior high and high school. He filled a void that was there in my life when I needed it.

However, make no mistake, he treated me like a little brother. When I was little, he mostly ignored me, but there were times I endured the taunting that little brothers have had to put up with since the beginning of time. I will not even discuss the nicknames my brother had for me.

I was usually the focus of his teasing and one event has stuck with me since the early 70s.

One of my sister's classmates had a younger sister and she had a nickname. People called her "Sailor" because she wore a sailor hat around town. Now, I had absolutely no interest in this girl, but my brother would tease me about her.

One day I was playing board games with some of my friends in the living room of our house. When suddenly, I hear this song start playing on our stereo… "Kiss me sailor, before you walk out the door…" It was a song that was made popular in 1964 by Diane Renay. For some reason, my mom bought the record and my brother discovered it and used it to taunt me for the next few years. Anytime he wanted to get me riled up, he would put on that song. Many times, he would choose to do this in front of my friends and I would try to get the record away from him. Every time I tried to get to the record, my brother would hold me back with his arm. I would be doing everything I could but he was too big for me. He loved to embarrass me. It is what brothers do. He would continue to tease me unmercifully with it until one day I was able to find where he hid the record. I broke it in half and threw it in the trash.

A few days later, I was once again playing with my friends in the living room when suddenly, I hear the start of "Kiss Me Sailor" on the record player. But this time it sounded different because my brother had found the record and tried to tape and glue it back together. Well… he did a good job because it would play long enough to get to the first line of the song and it would skip like a modern-day disc jockey when he "scratches" at the club. The first line of the song would start with… "K-k-k-k-k-kiss M-m-m-m-m-me S-s-s-s-s-sailor" over and over in an endless, embarrassing loop. I am not sure I ever heard my brother laugh so hard.

I have no idea whatever happened to that record. I wish I would have kept it. I must confess, as I write this, I am playing the song through my headphones. Tears fill my eyes, not because of the torment and the teasing I endured but because it has been such a topic of family conversations over the years. It takes me back to a younger me and I so wish I could tell that little boy to relax. It was a joke and it wouldn't last. I held on to the anger and I allowed it to fester for far too long.

My brother Bobby, was so different than me. I was born loving sports and he was born loving the outdoors. He loved animals, fishing, hunting and trapping. He always had a pet of some kind… even if my mom knew it or not. We shared a bedroom, but I have no memories of he and I specifically doing something together apart from playing records together and playing bedroom basketball.

I don't remember him being mean to me and for the most part he stayed out of trouble. Except for the time I remember he got in deep trouble for spray painting "The Glass of '74" on the train trestle on Park Street. No… that is not a typo, he wrote "The Glass of '74"… maybe in his excitement his C's looked a lot like G's. It stayed up there for a long time before they power washed it off the trestle.

I was close to my sister, Linda. She was protective of me when I was little and most of the happy memories I have from living on Walnut Street are in some way related to her. My sister went before me in school and my reputation began wherever hers left off. That doesn't mean it was easy. Here's how it worked for me, on the first day of class the teacher would do a roll call and would pause before they would say my name. They'd look up and say, "Any relation to Linda Lee?," I'd say, "Yes," and then the teacher would inform me and the entire class that my sibling is a perfect human specimen that I could never live up to.

However, I have clear evidence that she wasn't perfect. Most people didn't know it but she would torment her little brother with a prank or two. Probably the most significant one is when she and her girlfriends decided to pull a good one on me on a school night. My sister liked to have one of her girlfriends spend the night as she was growing up. It did not matter if it was a school night, it seemed to me like it was every night. Whether it was Lenora, Cindy, Sue, Pam or any number of other girls, like most 12-year-old boys, I never really minded having these cute older girls stay over.

One night when she had a few girls stay over, I was asleep in my bedroom and suddenly I am awakened by my sister and her friends telling me to get up. I needed to get moving if I was going to get to school on-time. So, I got up and sleepily went into my normal morning routine. I stumbled down the stairs and made my way into the kitchen. I got out the cereal and milk and was enjoying a bowl of Alpha-Bits before I would get dressed for school. I pour out another small bowl of cereal when I hear the laughter from my sister and her girlfriends, giggling and laughing, in the kitchen door way. I look up and see the clock and it is 2:00 AM.

I was livid and embarrassed. It took me a while to get over that one.

My siblings all say that I was the favorite in the eyes of my mother because I was the baby of the family. However, make no mistake, I paid a heavy price for being the "favorite". They would go out of their way to make sure I was firmly aware of my place in their eyes.

I should probably make an addition to my family story. My cousin, Larry, moved in with us shortly after his sophomore year. He grew up in Fort Wayne, Indiana and was the son of my dad's sister. Larry had a challenging upbringing. As I was told, he was always in trouble. Sometimes by the choices he made and other times by circumstances he could not control. Either way, he came to live with us shortly before the 1969-70 school year.

My mom took Larry in and he shared a bedroom with my brother Bobby and me. I immediately gravitated to Larry because even though I was nine years younger than him, he always treated me like a friend and not like a little brother. He would take me with him when he would go cruising around in his black Chevy Corvair and I loved that.

I was with my mom and Larry when she received the official paperwork from the Port Clinton Courthouse that granted her legal guardianship over him. I remember how happy Larry was about that.

Larry fit in with our family and looking back, I think he finally found a place where he felt he belonged. In the year or so that he lived with us he made a tremendous improvement with his grades and was set to graduate in the spring of 1971.

I guess you could say that my family appeared like any other family in the 1960's. However, at times, I am sure we were "dysfunctional." I struggle with the word "dysfunctional" and sometimes I substitute the word "non-traditional" when I talk about my family as if somehow, I could make life easier for all of us if I did not use such a harsh word. That by using this term, "non-traditional" I would give the indication that our life was something more of a burden or that it would hide the fact that all of us have hidden scars that have done damage in our lives. As much as I would like to deny that this was not the case, I cannot turn away from the fact that we do indeed have "scars" from our upbringing. So, even before the word became cliché, like many other families around us, we were at times dysfunctional.

Despite having an absent father, my brothers and sister experienced some of the joys of life. The thrill of growing up in innocence and the memories of Christmas mornings were magical. We weren't poor. I have seen poor in my life and that would not have best described us. On the other hand, we were not rich either. No silver spoons to eat with, just the lower level of Middle America. We never owned the house that we lived in, yet my dad always had a new car in the driveway.

We did not get the latest and greatest new toy that some children got on our block, at least not when they were most popular. The clothes that we wore were clean and appropriate. My sister had it somewhat easier when it came to clothes. I would have to endure the chore of wearing hand me downs from my brother Bobby. I am sure he had to wear clothes from our oldest brother Jim. We were not deprived of having "things" in our life. We were just on the "wait until school starts" plan for new clothes and the Christmas and Birthday wish list for toys. I can still smell the new clothes I received from the JC Penney catalog for the first day of school and I remember that life was no better, then when I got a "transistor radio" for my birthday when I was about eight.

Yet, as children, we acknowledged the pain that this life can give. We had our share of fights, broken bones, stitches and bumps and bruises. We experienced the ache of disappointment when we lost, the pangs of hurt over rejection and the sorrow of losing loved ones. We had our share of burdens… we have our own successes and failures, hurts, letdowns, and disappointments.

Sure, we survived them, but I cannot get away from the fact that this home on Walnut Street is such a huge part of my story. This house is where I grew up as a small child, it was where I spent my formative years, from kindergarten to middle-school. It's where I have the clearest memories of my family. This house became a memory box, storing moments of my life in each crevice and corner. In every memory of that house, I can see old scenes play out in front of me, fuzzy and transparent, like images on an old projector.

I see the sofa, where we used to watch tv together on Sunday nights. The kitchen table, where I sat side-by-side with my brothers and sister eating dinner together. The bedroom, where I shared a bed with my brother. Familiar images flickering like ghosts in the living room, in the kitchen, on the staircase, and in the hallways. It was home.

As I would look out the front window, I felt as if the whole world was right there. The boundaries of my neighborhood were defined by how far I could see. The axis upon which earth rotated, I was convinced that it was located somewhere in the alley that separated the Lee and Blakely households. The safe confines of this small-town America were the only boundaries I ever knew. For most of my adolescent years, nothing else existed past the signs that marked the edge of town. More importantly, the fact that for most of my young life, nothing really mattered past those signs as well.

This was indeed the center of the universe and everything that happened revolved around that place. It was my neighborhood. It was my world and it was all wrapped up in the security of living in a place and time where there really wasn't anything to fear. All the people and all the houses that surrounded you were as familiar as the things in your own room. It seemed magical and most people were not aware of what it really meant to have such a place to live in. I guess I wasn't aware of it then, amid the school plays, home cooked meals and the sounds of children playing in the backyard, but life was rich there.

When I was twelve, the owners of our Walnut Street home decided that they wanted to sell it. They offered it to my parents to buy, but my dad did not want to. For him, I guess, it was just a place to sleep on weekends. For us, it was a different story. This was our home. When my mom told me that we were going to move across town (albeit to a house five minutes away), a plethora of emotions fought for my attention. I was filled with grief for the familiar rooms that would no longer be mine. I felt cheated. I felt that my childhood memories were easily discarded, but I was desperate to cling to the house and the history. Inside, I was so upset over the decision to get rid of our comfortable old house and start over. Truth be told, I did not understand. These same memories that I was clinging to, were the same memories that my mom was trying to process as well. She had to make some decisions and this one was hard on all of us.

So, we moved away from our Walnut Street home and took up residence on Locust Street. When we closed the door behind us for the last time, even as a sixth grader, I was struck with the disconcerting notion that I would never be held by something in quite the same way again for a long time. I would be well into my adult years before I would ever live in a house that I considered "home." The other houses that I have lived in, have simply been a place to lay my head.

Today, however, the house where I now live, has been my home. I tried to give my children a place that they could consider "home." I wanted them to have what I had all those years ago. Over the years, my wife and I could have moved from the house where we raised four children with only one bathroom. We even made plans to do so, but there are reasons we didn't.

One reason is because of a door jamb in our kitchen. A door jamb where pencil marks measure the growth of a family. Each mark a memory and each mark with a date written beside it to note the growth. This door jamb tells the story of children growing up and becoming adults. These marks will remain on that door jamb until one day the new owners of our home decide to paint over them and make marks of their own.

Another reason why we have not moved is that the walls of our home speak to me. In the quiet, I can hear the echoes of our children laughing. I hear the chatter of them having friends over for movie nights. I hear the noise of birthday parties, of long talks at the dinner table, and the precious sounds of Christmas celebrations. I can still hear the click of the door closing behind my kids when they were out at night. That wonderful sound that they were home, safe and secure.

The walls of our home emit sounds of a family that was trying to find their way in this life. It surely wasn't perfect but the wonderful sounds that come from the walls of our home, far out-weigh any noise of discord that there may have been. In time, these wonderful sounds will fade. Many are already being replaced by the laughter and the banter of our grandsons playing in the living room.

Eventually, we will move from this home. Maybe someday, years from now, my children will come back and drive past this home. Maybe they will find the nerve to walk up to the front door, and knock. A stranger will open it, and they'll explain that they used to live here, in this very house, a long time ago and maybe, just maybe, they'll let them in.

5

THE GIFT OF FRIENDSHIP

*I*f you are not recognized in the eyes of your local community, the chances that your passing will even be noticed are slim. If your accomplishments are quiet accomplishments, cherished by only by those who love you, likely you go and leave this world in silence.

Your death will be just a blurb in the local obituary. People will read your name and think it sounds familiar but really can't remember anything significant about you. They skim the obit, and most will not even read the whole thing, and quickly move on to the comics and the sports pages. The newspaper gets thrown out with the trash that week. The obituary that represents a life lived will be disregarded and life moves on.

It happens every single day. A life lived among people in their community that hardly ever gets recognized. But if you are lucky, and I mean really lucky, you find a few friends that you will hold close even in death. Friends who mean everything to you. Friends without whom our lives would have been empty. Friends who are enduring models of grace and good fortune of having them in our life.

When we lose them in death... and we all do, we all will... we realize, then and forever, that our own lives have been filled with the precious gift that they have given us. The gift of friendship. A gift of love that can only be found in authentic friendship. It's so rare to have this in your life.

If you are fortunate to still have someone in your life that is truly your first friend... your oldest friend, then you must consider yourself extremely blessed. Especially if they remain your friend and close to you no matter where in the world leads you. You don't have to live in the same cities, you don't have to see each other on a daily or even monthly basis. True friendships, especially old friendships, don't require that.

No one would ever know you better. No one in your adult life saw you the way you were in the beginning. The way you were before the inevitable defenses were put up to protect you from this thorny world. Before you constructed the layers of protective walls. You didn't invite or ask these defenses to be a part of your life. You didn't willingly participate in the building of these walls in your life. They sneak up on you and they come, like a thief in the night, whether you like it or not. It's included in the package. It's documented in the fine small print of the terms and conditions of this thing we call life. All of us have someone who was there before these walls.

I am one of the lucky ones. I have had this kind of true friendship a handful of times in my life. Three of those people have now passed on. All three left this world way too young and I am left alone with their memory and a clipping of their obituary from the local newspaper. I acknowledge that my life would have had little meaning if not for that one day when our lives connected and we would become treasured friends.

Bryan Blakely was my first true friend. There wasn't much that we didn't do together in those early years, especially during the summer when our time was spent outside. Heroic battles of war and epic athletic feats of football and baseball were commonplace in the yard that made up our playground.

In the mid-1960's, at least in this pocket of Northwest Ohio, mothers who were stay-at-home housewives were the rule, working mothers were the exception. My mother would have peanut butter and jelly sandwiches ready for us; his mother always had cookies and snacks available. We would drink Kool-Aid by the gallon and we would only come in long enough to refuel and get back to the battle that was waiting for us outside.

Out on the well-worn paths of Blakely's yard, we might have

fooled ourselves into thinking we were NFL stars or maybe one day play baseball in the major leagues. Some days, there was even the possibility that we were just combatting soldiers who, when the battle was over, returned not to foxholes or mud-splattered tents, but to chocolate-chip cookies and milk just a few feet from the battlefield.

It was a feeling that we accepted and appreciated. We understood it very well in the deceptively quiescent middle-class life in the mid-sixties. Life was full of possibilities and dreams. We were still sheltered from the stark reality of what life would bring in the coming years.

As I think back on those times, I can only consider it was more than just blind luck to have met Bryan and his family. If you consider the influence and impact on my life, I believe that it was part of a greater design that came from a place much bigger and more powerful other than it just being "blind luck". The Blakely family was such a part of my life that there were times when the lines of who was my immediate family sometimes blurred for me.

Ray and Jeni Blakely had four sons. Mike the oldest, followed by Mark, then Bryan, with Keith being the youngest. I didn't have as close a relationship with Mike. He was older, and I was just too young and was probably more of a nuisance to him. Just like I was to my brother Jim. Mike was a hard worker and always seemed to be busy at something. I always looked up to Mike.

Mark Blakely was just a few years older than me and I have always had a close friendship with him. Mark hung out with my brother Bobby more often than with me. He's got scars to prove it too. One of my brother Bobby's favorite places to hang out and play wasn't Blakely's yard. It was a small creek that connected to the Portage River. This creek ran next to the local cemetery and under the bridge on State Route 105. This was probably more fun for my brother than it was for Mark, but they would swing over a fence and climb down to the water where they would play. They would look for snakes, catch crawfish or any other animal they could find. Eventually, they would make their way up the creek to investigate the echoes under the bridge. They would stand under the road while cars drove above them. Soon they would get bored and head home but it wouldn't take long before they would find themselves on another adventure like this one. On one occasion, as they played in the creek, Mark seriously cut his foot on something in the water and received stitches as a result. I must admit that they are not the only stitches that were earned by the activities of the Lee's and Blakely's. It came with the territory, and we knew it was worth the risk of just hanging out with each other. However, one day a few months after this incident, Mark made a decision to not "hang" out with my brother and it saved his life.

Keith was the youngest and he was the quietest. I did not know Keith as well as the other boys. Keith was a loner and usually kept to himself. Keith was always around, usually playing or doing something by himself, but every now and then he would get involved with our games and outside activities. As a child, he always seemed distant and hard to get to know. When I was young, I did not know what Keith struggled with and though I would eventually find out, we were friends, just not as close as I was with Bryan.

I never really got to know Ray, Bryan's dad. When I first met Ray he was a truck driver, like my father. For me, he wasn't around much and he would eventually become a successful businessman and own buildings and businesses in our town.

Jeni Blakely accepted me as one of her own from the first moment I met her. She treated me accordingly. On certain levels, Jeni Blakely was as much a mom to me and Mike, Mark, Bryan and Keith were as much brothers to me as my own.

I remember the exact moment I became friends with Bryan. He was a year older than me. He was wise to the world as only a six-year-old can be. He was funny, out-going and very sure of himself.

I wasn't any of those things.

One of my favorite memories of him was the first Halloween that he and I could go door-to-door with each other. We were given very strict instructions on what our boundaries were. We were so excited and when the time came we bolted out the door and headed down Walnut Street to take in our haul of candy. I realize that being confined to the ten houses that lined our street was a bit limiting. However, it could have been New York City as far as we were concerned.

I am sure, in the darkness, our mothers were following closely behind hoping to not get caught checking on us. In today's world, I would not allow my six-year-old grandson to go off my front porch without me holding his hand to ensure that nothing would happen to him. But this was 1966. It was a different time and place.

I dressed as a pirate, in a black costume that came with a beard, a hat, and an eye-patch. If I really concentrate, I can still smell the chemicals that were part of the beard that covered my face. It was probably made from the same material that was used to make rocket fuel. I remember that after the night was over, my face was covered by red splotches because of the beard. But I wouldn't take it off for anything. I was a pirate with an eye patch and a hook. I was loving every minute of it. Bryan was dressed as a ghost, with a draped bedsheet over his head with the eyes cut out by his mom for him to see.

Off we went with our pillowcase in hand to collect all the candy we would haul in for the night. Bryan and I would ring each doorbell, politely informing each person who answered that we were there to either get a treat or we would have to trick them. Up and down the street were kids we played with every day. It was a slow-moving parade of princesses, cheerleaders, hobos, football players, cowboys, gangsters and one pirate and one bed-sheet ghost.

Our mothers less than fifty-feet away… even if we knew it or not.

I have no tangible proof that these events happened other than the vivid memories in my mind. I regret that there are no pictures of our costumes or of us sitting on the living room floor at the end of the night emptying our pillowcases to admire our pile of candy. There are no pictures of us spending the next hour or so trading each other for our favorite candies, all the while stuffing our face with the fruit of our spoils.

As I have mentioned before, I have no doubt that the alleyway which ran between Walnut and Washington Street was the exact location of the axis in which the world revolved around. From the time I was four-years-old, to the age of fifteen, the center of my world was found on that alley. Every day during the summer, the first thing I would do was head out the door and make my way over that alley to the Blakely's, to the adventure awaiting me for that day.

Back in the day, we didn't sit in front of the TV or a computer playing games. Most days we would leave the house in the morning and not come back until the street lights came on. That was the unwritten rule, we could go wherever we wanted until the street lights came on. Many times, we would eat lunch where ever we were. That is how it was. No matter where we were, or what friend's house we were near, it always seemed we would just eat lunch there. During the day, the town limit signs was the boundary. After the lights came on, we were confined to the neighborhood. Which was perfect because we would play until it was so dark we couldn't see our hands in front of our face. Many nights of hide and seek, tag and catching lightning bugs.

The only fear we had in life was getting home after the street lights came on. There would be hell to pay if you did not report in when the lights came on. Whether it was my mom or Bryan's mom we would get "in trouble" if we didn't get home as soon as the lights came on.

How did we leave the house at 8:00 AM and not show up sometimes until those lights come on? The only answer was that during those early years we were raised by mom's that took the parental path of least resistance. Bryan's mom, Jeni, had the "right" to discipline me, just as my mom had the same right to discipline Bryan. Other than the both of us having a smart mouth and a tendency to talk back to them, neither one of our moms had to intervene very much.

Not that they neglected us — far from it. But they never over-supervised. They let us have our freedom — freedom to bike, freedom to play, freedom to gash our heels open and leave a trail of blood up the sidewalk. This wasn't seen as particularly dire, by the way; they just bandaged us up and we went back outside. We had bikes and we rode them — fast, alone, in the middle of the street, and on the sidewalks.

If I gave my children the kind of freedom we had back in the mid-sixties, someone would have called social services. My children would never have the luxury of riding alone on their bicycle as they pedaled as fast as they could down the sidewalk or jumping over curbs and going anywhere they wanted to.

If I had a wish for my adult children, it would be that they would have the opportunity to parent like my mom did. That they would have the ability to let my grandchildren roam, and bike, and splash in strange creeks. I want them to see snakes, not know if they're venomous, and run screaming. I want them to peel the skin off their knee when they hit a mailbox on their bicycle. And yes, I want them to slash their heel, and scrape their elbows, and throw rocks when no one is looking. Sometimes the best part of growing up are the times when no one is watching. Our moms gave us marvelous freedoms; I wish I could give the same to my grandchildren.

Our moms let us roam the neighborhood. It was never as big a space as we remember it to be, but we could go and truly play outside. We didn't have an air conditioner, and on hot days the coolest place to be was outside. If we didn't feel like going to the pool we'd ride our bikes several blocks across town to Veteran's Park where we'd swing on the swings and hang upside down on the monkey bars. There were seesaws and we would promise that we wouldn't jump off them to cause the other to come crashing down to the ground. We would lie and eventually one of us would jump off and laugh as the other end of the seesaw would crash down in a freefall. It caused more than one fight on those summer afternoons.

There was the old merry-go-round that regularly either dragged us through the mud or launched us off as a projectile. We would spin it as fast as we could and desperately hold on for our lives. We usually lost our ability to hold on and the launch mode of the merry-go-round would go into effect. When we grew older, we would talk about this and joke that this would be the time of our lives when we learned to "tuck and roll".

More than once, we would talk each other out of "telling" on each other or to not report an injury that we earned because of our lack of common sense. The bruises and cuts were just evidence of a friendship that would outlast them. They were nothing more than what a healthy dose of Mercurochrome couldn't cure.

Now, truth be told, even then, we had well-meaning adults that would ask where our parents were. After all, most every other child at the park would have a parent pushing their kids on the swing, or sitting on the seesaw, or slowly turning the merry-go-round with dire warnings to "Hold on!" I am sure that when they would see us coming they'd mutter under their breath and debate whether to call our parents or the police. Either way, when we would show up many times it was, according to those well-meaning parents, "time" for them to go home and we would have the run of the park.

When we would grow tired, we would ride our bikes uptown to see what was going on. We bought candy by the fistful at the W.R. Thomas 5-10 store. All that sugar would fuel late-night sleepover conversations. I am reminded of the arctic chill of Blakely's basement floor and how we'd seek refuge from the summer heat by spreading our sleeping bags out over the floor. With the lights turned off, there was just enough glow from the black and white, three-channel TV for our time of telling stories and lies to each other.

Tucked in a sleeping bag on a cold basement floor, summer nights had the effect of a sacred place. We would talk about our plans for the next day, told scary stories and made fun of each other to make ourselves feel better. That would cross the line somewhere along the conversation and we would have a fight every now and then.

Midnight felt so late and so adult.

Sometimes, as we fought to keep our eyes open to see who could stay up the latest and after we would hear that familiar yell come down the stairwell "to keep it quiet down there" we would then start the conversations of our dreams and what we would become when we got older.

We would talk until our conversations drifted off into sleep. In the morning, none of us would dare talk about our late-night conversations. We knew that any further discussion in the light of day would jinx the possibilities. It was a pact that we believed but never discussed. It all felt surreal, and for now, our dreams were safe from the rocks of reality. Protected from the light of day, forever stowed away with the moon.

Looking back at the friendship that Bryan and I had all those years ago, I wish I would have known the exact morning that Bryan and I would play outside as young kids, sheltered from the outside world, for the last time.

Everyone will experience this. It is a fact of life.

Bryan and I got up one morning and played outside. It was a day just like the day before. The difference was that we did not realize that this one specific day would be the last time. As the sun strained to yield the last rays of light, our intentions were set on doing it all again tomorrow. However, in the stealth of night, in the peaceful sleep of two boys who were the best of friends, a page would be turned and it would forever change. We would remain friends for years, but the sad truth is that there always is a "last time." Sadly... neither one of us knew it.

I have wonderful memories of a time in my life that was surrounded by the innocence of living in a small town in the sixties. Had I known that it wouldn't last, had I known which day would be the last time we would play as innocent children, I would have taken time to savor it. I would have fought harder to remain there. I would have paused and acknowledged that it would be the last time we would ever have it that good.

One of that last times I hung out with him was a time that we walked home from the fair when we were 16. We had just spent the last night of the fair walking around checking out the girls and just having a good time. Nothing of significance happened that evening at the fair.

Just the two of us acting stupid, (and again) trying to be cool.

We failed.

Things change so fast in life.

I tried to act as if we were on the same path, but I knew I was fooling myself. I hadn't told Bryan that I made some decisions that would change our ability to hang out together. It was one thing to be in different classes, but now we would be going to different schools, in different towns.

There would come a time when there was something in the air when we would get together. We would try to recreate the past, but it was never the same. There always seemed to be something foreign and unwelcome in the air. We were veering off into different directions and we could not stop the change that was happening. We no longer hung out in the basement. We no longer talked every day. We no longer needed each other that way.

I just couldn't help but think of who we once were. Two kids that would spend hours walking around town at all hours of the night, talking about everything under the sun. Two kids that would spend hours tossing rolled up socks into a basket above the bedroom door. We didn't know back then what was waiting for us. We didn't know who we would become.

It happens to everyone, everything changes. It's what the world does to all of us and we can do nothing to stop it from happening.

Forty years later, I would speak at his funeral. He would leave this world too soon and I would be left to finish this life without the best friend of my childhood. I had known him for over 45 years and from the age of 5 to 16, I cannot think of one thing that I was a part of that he wasn't involved in, in some way. He and I played together and fought together. We were life-long friends.

I miss him more as the years pass. I would love to have more conversations and tell stories to each other about growing up together. I would love to thank him for being there for me when I most needed it. I would love to tell him, once again, that we didn't have to be related by blood to be brothers.

To this very day, I have a picture in a small frame sitting on my home office desk. In that frame is a small faded picture of me and Bryan. I look at that picture every single day of my life. The picture was taken just before we picked up our dates for the Homecoming Dance in 1975.

We were desperately trying to look cool in our leisure suits and long hair.

And once again, we failed.

6

WHEN A.M. RADIO WAS KING

*B*ryan was always a step ahead of me when it came to music. Even at the age of eight or nine, he liked his music to be harder. We called it "hard rock" and I wasn't a fan. At that time, I still liked the sappy love/pop songs of the era. The Archie's, "Sugar, Sugar" and "Dizzy" by Tommy Roe was about as "hard" as I liked my music. As a matter of fact, I knew the music catalog of The Monkee's better than that of The Beatles.

For my eighth birthday in 1969, my mom gave me a portable AM transistor radio. I was thrilled. Everyone I knew wanted one. My radio was six inches by four inches or so, ran on a 9-volt battery, came with a brown leather carrying case, and most important, a white bakelite single earphone. I wish I could remember the brand. There were days when I carried my radio with me everywhere I went outside of school hours, and that earphone was in my ear from the time I got up until I left for school, and after I arrived home from school until I fell asleep at night.

So many times, when we think of our childhood memories, we think of friends, family and the events that surrounded us. It might have been playing baseball, swimming at the lake, going to Cedar Point or just hanging out with your friends in the neighborhood.

For me, many of my childhood memories were filled with sound. When I hear these "sounds" today, I am instantly taken back in my

41

mind to the 1960s and 70s. I can remember memories and I can go back to where I was when I first heard it. I can smell the chlorine in Teagarden's pool or the smell the freshly mowed grass of the field all my friends and I played on. These special sounds… were the sounds of Motown Music.

In those days, long before FM Stereo, the only radio station that was of importance was CKLW out of Detroit / Windsor, Ontario, Canada. "The BIG 8" as it was called back then. It was a loud, glitzy noise-making radio. Everything was shouted — even the news. The 50,000-watt AM radio giant spewed rock and roll and hyped-news across 28 states and mid-Canada. It broadcast from across the Detroit River in Windsor, Ontario, but it was Detroit's station. I will never forget the tagline that the DJ's would say, "C-K-L-W, The Motor Cit-eeeee." The capital of the music world was not Nashville, nor was it Los Angeles. Back then, it was Detroit, Michigan.

The style… the sound… the hits.

It was Motown. It was everywhere, and it was ours.

I have clear memories of long summer nights spent listening to music. I carry that Motown sound in my musical tastes even to this day. All I do is put some music on from that era, close my eyes, and suddenly I am drawn back to the times when all of us listened to music on our dime-store AM transistor radios.

We had not yet experienced the stereo sound of FM channels. That would come in the coming years, but back then, we were content to have our musical tastes defined by AM radio stations. There were only a handful of AM stations that you could tune in to during the day and most of those stations went off the air when the sun went down. When we would tire of CKLW, we would try to get channels that you couldn't tune in during the day and if the weather was right and the wind blew in the right direction, sometimes you could bring in other stations. If you had a transistor radio, you knew that there was a special niche in getting your favorite station to come in. Sometimes you had to hold it just at the right angle and maybe above your head to hear your favorite channel.

One summer day, Bryan and I were riding our bikes around the neighborhood when he said that we should put in our earphone and tune into the same station. That way we could listen to music as we rode around. It was brilliant! I had no idea why we had not thought of it before. So, that is what we did. We put in our earphone and soon all our buddies were doing the same thing.

All of us riding our bikes around town with the mono earphone blasting in our ear. If the music sounded tinny on the main speaker of the radio, the headphone earpiece was much worse, but we felt cool and we would listen to the same music as we rode around town. It was like living our own version of a music video.

One day, I guess the sheer fear of the potential "gang" violence coming from a group of adolescent bicycle riders wearing an earphone in town caught the attention of the police of our small town. The "gang" of five from our neighborhood was riding in the unfamiliar territory of Erie and Portage Streets. As far as we were concerned, it could have been as far away as Toledo to us. The corner of Erie and Portage was not a place where we would frequent. But there was a feeling of strength in numbers and all five us rode with no fear of attack from a rival "gang."

We were just passing time, trying to escape the boredom of a hot sunny day. Our parents would have been upset at us for being so far from our block. I am not sure exactly why we were over there, it was probably because of a girl. That was usually the motivation for much of the things we would do. We were riding in circles and just hanging out on a street corner that wasn't familiar to us.

No mischief, nor ill will towards anyone.

Then we saw the police car coming down the street towards us. All of us, for some reason, knew that they were coming to ask us what we were doing so far away from our own turf.

Back then, our small town had just a few police officers. Most kids only knew the name of the chief and one other officer. That officer was Larry St. Clair. Larry seemed to know everyone and always had the reputation of being "cool" and fair whenever he had to deal with something.

I looked at Bryan and said, "I hope it's Larry St. Clair."

It wasn't.

It was the police chief, Bill Paulsen.

Now by all accounts, Bill Paulsen was a wonderful man, a good man. Someone who dedicated his entire life to protecting the small-town of Oak Harbor, Ohio. I'm sure he knew all of us by name and knew we were not going to be the cause of any trouble. However, this was the late 1960s, and there was a certain aptitude for standing up against authority figures. So, we fought the immediate urge to flee and sat defiantly on the banana seats of our stingray bikes, waiting to hear what "the man" had to say.

He had a job to do and he pulled up next to us and said, "What's going on boys?"

Boys!?! Did he just call us boys? While the fact remains that we were, in fact, "boys," we were at the point that anything that came out of his mouth we would have found something wrong with it. Even though we thought ourselves to be bad and rebellious, we would never show outward disrespect.

We simply responded, "nutin" to his question.

"What brings you to this side of town?" he asked inquisitively.

Bryan responded with clarity, "Nothing… just riding our bikes."

Chief Paulsen paused for a moment to look at us and make a mental picture of who was lined up in our "gang."

"Well, boys, behave yourself," he replied as he started to pull away.

He suddenly stopped his car and said that maybe riding around town with our earphone in one ear wasn't safe, so it was a good idea to put it away while we were riding our bikes.

Bryan defiantly rolled his eyes as Chief Paulsen continued his safety lecture. The rest of us all disconnected the wire, wrapped it around the radio and stuffed it in our pockets. Bryan was the last to comply.

Chief Paulsen waited until all of us put our radios away. Bryan waited all of 10 seconds after the Chief drove away to put his back on. He was always a rebel when it came to those sorts of things. We quickly followed his lead. We pulled our radios from our pockets and one-by-one, turned the AM radio on and put the earphone back in our ear. We all looked each other in the eye like we were the Hell's

Angels motorcycle gang. We knew that the police never bothered us on our own turf. We gave each other a head nod, never spoke a word and took off again on our bicycle journey. Our unspoken quest was to ride across town, back to the confines of the safe zone of our neighborhood without getting caught by the "fuzz" or Chief Paulsen.

In reality, Chief Paulsen wasn't chasing us. He probably never gave us a second thought after he pulled his car away. But, fueled by our active imagination and an attempt to create some drama to kill the boredom, we now had a quest and a story we would talk about for years.

Each of us was on our own to find any way possible to get back to "home" base.

Suddenly, we split up and each one of us was zipping down separate alleys and sidewalks... riding our bikes through backyards and boulevards, all in the quest to get home.

Bryan was the first to arrive back at our home base in the alley between Walnut and Washington Streets. I was the second gang member to get there and we waited patiently for the others to return. It was like waiting for soldiers to return from the battlefield, hoping they would report to the command center, but knowing it did not end well for them if they didn't show up soon.

I remember whooping and hollering as a group when everyone made it back. We defied "the man" and we weren't just boys on bikes that could be bossed around. We leapt off our bikes and were jumping around like we just won the World Series. We patted each other on the back, gave each other hugs and looked each other in the eye with the acknowledgment that we were forever tied together by this single act of defiance.

No longer boys... but men.

We were hardcore.

We were a gang.

We were rebels... rebels without a clue.

That was how that summer progressed. We were no longer bound to the alley between Walnut and Washington Streets. We were gaining some independence and our music was changing too.

On one of the many sleepovers that summer, we were down in Bryan's basement discussing music. We would always have music playing and we would sometimes act as if we were the artist singing. This night we were talking about the song, "Crimson and Clover" by Tommy James and The Shondells. Bryan was trying to explain to me how the song was made and all the benefits of the sound of stereo music.

As we grew older, Bryan would be the one to introduce me to stereo FM music. He was the first of my friends to have a record player that played stereo music and had an FM radio receiver attached to it. Suddenly, music was about listening to albums. I was introduced to bands like Aerosmith, KISS, The Edgar Winter Group, The Doobie Brothers, Black Sabbath, Jethro Tull, Grand Funk, Bad Company and Deep Purple. In front of Bryan, I always told him I liked the music he was exposing me to, but deep down when I would turn on my transistor radio, I would always turn on CKLW and listen to Motown and the sappy pop songs on AM radio.

I am a child of a time when AM radio was king.

No offense to anyone reading this... but if you never listened to AM radio on a transistor radio you probably will not understand the significance of this period of history. It's not your fault, you just don't know that you were cheated out of a great time period in music history.

For me, it was always wrapped up in the music. Saturday mornings were spent watching cartoons and the afternoons were spent watching American Bandstand so you could see the latest dance moves and possibly your favorite singer or band.

It was the decade of The Beatles, Dylan, Aretha, The Beach Boys, The Rolling Stones, and Zeppelin. But that's not all it was. The 1960s also included The Monkee's, The Kinks, Creedence Clearwater Revival and The Jackson Five. While my sister was enamored with Donnie Osmond and my brother was into Steppenwolf, I was all about The Temptations, The Four Tops, Smokey Robinson, The Supremes and Stevie Wonder just to name a few.

It was a single-oriented era—a startlingly inventive period following the initial explosion of rock'n'roll but before the album became dominant—when entire new genres seemed to bubble up every few months. The 1960s marked a time when pop music became more than a teenage fad. Music was turning into an important art form as it sound tracked the civil rights movement, the hippie heyday, and the Vietnam War.

I've wondered what it must look like to the younger generations who didn't live through the 60s. Are they awe-struck by the moon landing? Is teetering on the verge of nuclear war just the start of a good sci-fi movie? Are the assassinations of political and human right leaders just names and dates to memorize for a history exam? Were the hippies, flower power, Woodstock, the Vietnam War, women's lib, civil rights, the space race, the Cold War, the British Invasion, TANG, miniskirts, Charles Chips, bell bottoms, lava lamps, tie dyed t-shirts, Green Stamps, Evel Knievel - and who could forget the Manson murders - just evidence of a random decade? I think not. The list could go on and on.

It's inevitable that all of us would see when AM radio was king through our own personal lens. The 60's and 70's were like an epic blockbuster that involved music, clothes, politics, social unrest and social change. There really hasn't been anything like it since. So many historic events happened in that period.

But that doesn't mean that I want to go back.

History has a knack for showing the flaws of a generation that planted the seeds to produce it.

That's what all historians do; they look back and see things that were planted and the results of which may not be seen for years. While I love to look back and remember, it's important that we don't forget that many of the seeds that were planted all those years ago are the reasons we now see major political, social, and cultural changes in our society. We wonder how this generation of young people can be the way they are and truth be told it is because of the seeds that were planted in the 60's and 70's.

We have made the mistake of ignoring the seeds that we planted. In many ways we don't like the results, yet we are the ones to blame. Our children pay the price of not having the freedom we had to play outside and have the run of the town. We now dare not let our young children out of our sight for fear that they may one day have their picture on a milk carton. We thought we had it under control, yet we act as if the change itself remains unexpected, invisible, even unimaginable to most people. We should never forget how surprisingly fast these changes can happen.

Nevertheless, looking back at the seeds planted when AM radio was king is very important, because it can help us pay more attention to seeds that are growing underground right now. Of course, we can't predict which seeds will connect with which other ones to create significant change, and certainly not when or how it will happen. But history can teach us to watch more closely and optimistically for signs of change that might be coming surprisingly soon.

The seeds of change. I can fully appreciate how malleable history is and how its perspective changes with time. I imagine 40 years of perspective on any decade we've lived through would be interesting. Forty years from now, I'm confident that the Obama and Trump years will also look much different through the lens of history. I really regret that I probably won't be around to read it.

I enjoy U.S. History more than most, but in the years that have passed, I've forgotten more names and dates than I remember. Our history is complicated and imperfect. There are facets of it I don't fully understand.

It was all filtered by growing up in a small town. It was easy to find people who sneeringly complained about how trapped they felt there as a teenager. I was no different from most kids growing up there... I began making plans of escape early on, but I still got to experience the life of living in a small town when AM radio was king.

Oak Harbor held on to those days longer than most and that makes me smile even after all these years. But once the seeds of change are planted it is hard to ever go back to the way it used to be.

The history that was built for me was wrapped up in what we had when AM radio was king. It's gone now, and we will never get it back. We have future generations that will never fully understand what it was like back in those days.

That makes me incredibly sad and I will forever miss the days when A.M. radio was king.

7

A GENTLEMAN NEVER TELLS

I always thought I would marry a girl from Oak Harbor. It was something I always accepted. I never thought it would work out any other way. I never really looked elsewhere. I always assumed that I would find her, and we would marry and leave Oak Harbor for a while, but we would come back home to raise our kids. Our children would walk the same halls as we did in R.C. Waters Elementary School, they would play on the same little league teams and ultimately, they would be nurtured in the same environment as we were.

That wouldn't happen because that plan would change on an April day in 1976. The girl of my dreams would cross my path and from the moment I first laid eyes on her, I knew I had found my heart's desire. It took me awhile to convince her to have the same interest in me, but I wore her down until she went out with me. I guess I am lucky that my "persistence" didn't get me served with a restraining order. She has been my wife for many years and I am still a very lucky man.

But it didn't start out that way. My interest in girls started early and as the story goes, more than once, my mom had to retrieve me and my tricycle from a girl's house a block away. I don't remember doing this, but apparently, I would escape as often as I could.

One of the things that characterized and shaped my budding

social life in the days of elementary school was the concept of "liking" a girl. It was a topic of great interest to me and it always took up more of my attention than it ever should have. Notice that I say it took up more of my time, but I do not say anything about it taking up any time for the girls I was interested in. That's because most of the girls had no idea that I "liked' them. Many times, I was too shy or too scared to say anything to them. It would cause my stuttering to go out of control and my words would be a jumbled mess as they spilled from my mouth. So, I just never said a word.

However, each school year would start the same way. Within the first few days of school starting, the conversations at recess or in the lunch line, revolved around "who liked who" and who was "going steady" with whom. I always found the term, "going steady" a funny expression when it came to the pursuit of a relationship between two kids. They don't use the term "going steady" anymore. What exactly did it mean? Considering the filter of the 1960's, it meant that you "liked" someone and were "exclusive" in who you liked. There was not, in fact, anything at all proprietary in who you liked. It required no acknowledgment or even the knowledge of the person being liked, and any number of boys would like the same girl without antagonism. Most boys did like the same girl. It only became serious when you would cross the line and "go steady" for a few weeks.

While I had several "going steady" relationships throughout my elementary years, I have had two... yes, I said "two" relationships where the term "going steady" applied but I never had any direct verbal conversation between me and the other girl. Communication between the two of us took place only on handwritten notes. At no time during our torrid two-week relationship did we ever speak to each other. Maybe we would smile at each other and maybe you would get real bold a give her a head nod and have brief eye contact for a moment in time. The only physical contact between a couple was made during recess playing "tag." You could always tell the couples by who they chased during recess. It was innocent and harmless, but back in those days it seemed important and we took it seriously.

The notes of communication passed through the hands of trustworthy friends that would not embarrass you. The note would pass through no less than two boys and three girls as it made its way to the girl I was going "steady" with. The same path of communication would be directed back to me. Handwritten notes, folded in various ways, that would make even the professional origamist (a person who performs origami) proud. The more intricate the folds of the note indicated the level of "like" someone had for you. The tell-tale indicator of problems on the horizon was paying attention to the folds of the note that was passed on to you. A simple bi-fold note was a sure sign of a "Dear John" letter. I must admit that I received more than my fair share of bi-fold notes. I would be heartbroken for a few days and then my attention would drift to someone else and I would "like" them for a while. I was always waiting for the opportunity to find out from the rumor mill at recess or the lunch line if there was any interest from the other girl to "go steady."

Usually, there wasn't any interest.

I had mentioned earlier that many of the boys could "like" the same girl and there was never any doubt about which girl was the central figure of my elementary years. It was "Church Street." Now, before I confuse you with the name Church Street, let me clarify that I call her that name because I have no intention of ever saying her real name so that I don't embarrass her after all these years. It is just a term I use to reference her existence and I will never confirm that she ever lived on "Church Street." She has lived all her adult years without the knowledge or the reality of having me "like" her, she surely doesn't need the humiliation of me giving her name out and writing about it all these years later.

In my elementary years, the girl that drew the most attention was Church Street. It seemed obvious that she was oblivious to all the boys who liked her. However, it seemed to me that there was one boy that every now and then, would draw her attention. He was one of the few people that I must admit to having envied in my life. I always kept the secret from everyone, even friends, of the name of the one I really liked. I suppose I did that from not wanting to be a person entertaining false hopes, and the uncertainty as to what might be required of me should Church Street like me back. I don't know what I would have done had she showed any interest in me. I don't believe I would have been completely comfortable being around her. She was more mature and self-assured than I was at the time. I never made public my interest, I secretly joined most of the other boys in asserting the wishful title of "liking" Church Street.

The question of what "liking" a girl meant to me is not an easy one to answer now. I can't remember ever having a strong crush on Church Street. I would experience "crushes" in my life and that isn't what I felt towards her. I just really thought she was sharp and that she set the bar of what I "liked" in a girl. She was always nice to everyone and she always seemed so sure of herself and everyone wanted to be like her. At that time, I viewed her as the standard of what I wanted in a girlfriend. That standard would remain in place until I met Pam, who would one day become my wife. My wife would re-set the bar and she maintains that ideal to this very day. However, back then I was just trying to figure this whole boy-girl thing out. I knew boys liked girls and vice versa and that there was some silliness involved in the pairings, and that eventually one day, they would kiss and of course get married.

That was probably the depth of what I thought about "liking" a girl. I knew that my friends and I were fascinated by girls but none of us had any clue as to why. All of this is worth more contemplation, but there was a prestige that went with being liked by the prettier, higher status girls. And at the top of that list was Church Street.

Church Street lived in a house that I would find an excuse to ride my bike by every now and then. I would peddle my bike by just to see if she was there. If she was out on her porch, I would ride by and never give any indication that I even saw her. I would never dare to stop and talk to her. I would ride the loop and head back home to excitedly tell Bryan or one of my other friends that I saw her out on her porch. Mind you, she never acknowledged me or said anything to me as I would pass by her house, but for a few years, it was something that would make a dull day exciting.

During the summer, she spent time at Teagarden's pool and that was one of the reasons I made a point to go there every chance I could. Even if I didn't want to swim, I would go just because there was the probability that she might be there.

I must finally admit that I also called her constantly on the phone. Note: I did not say I talked to her on the phone. I'm merely pointing out the fact that I called her.

I grew up in a time when having a "telephone" was a pretty big deal. Back then having a telephone meant something entirely different than it does today. Our house had one of those Bakelite black rotary dial telephones. The phone didn't allow you to text and it surely did not have a camera.

Our phone was strategically placed in our kitchen. Which meant that every time it would ring, you had to get up from where you were and answer the phone in the kitchen. I remember it being heavy and I still remember the distinct extremely loud ring those phones used to have. The best part was that the phone made a funny clacking sound as you would dial up the number you needed to call.

For those of you reading this that have no idea what I am talking about, let me explain. Whenever I needed to make a call, I would pick up the handset and then stick my finger in the hole on that dial that represented the first digit of the phone number I wanted to call. Then I would spin the dial in a clockwise motion, producing in the process a satisfying "zzzzzttt!" noise. My finger would stop when it hit a small curved bar, I would then remove my finger and let the dial spin counterclockwise back to its resting position. I immediately repeated these steps for the next digit in the telephone number.

In that "get-off-the-phone" era of your mom standing next to you for your entire phone call because we only had one line into our house, there wasn't much freedom to extend past your five-minute allotted time limit. We had what you called back then a "party line" and having a "party line" was not as much fun as it sounded. Having a party line meant that you shared one phone line for pretty much your entire neighborhood. At any given time, you could go to the phone to make a call and someone would be on the line. This was always a frustration and it would a bigger problem if one of your neighbors would leave the phone off the hook. More than once my mom would send me over to our next-door neighbor, Mrs. Wheeler, to tell her to hang up her phone.

Another issue that you always had to deal with is that with a party line you could listen in on other people's calls. I learned the hard way about that. One day I picked up the phone and one of our neighbors was on the line. Now, most times the phone would make a clicking noise that would alert the people on the line that someone had picked up the phone and was potentially listening in on their conversation.

Occasionally, you could pick up the phone and the timing of the click would be covered by conversation and they would not be aware that someone was listening.

I picked up the phone and I was listening in on their conversation. I would like to say that I heard some deep and scandalous conversation, but that wasn't the case. Still, I was intrigued, and I stayed on the line. After about two minutes my mom walked into the kitchen and asked me who I was on the phone with. I hurriedly hung up the phone and she immediately knew that I had been listening in on someone else's phone call.

Nothing is more humiliating than having your mom pick up the phone to find out who was on the line and then make me walk over to that person's house and apologize face-to-face. Then I had to come home to face the punishment from my mother. Even though I continued to be tempted to listen in, I learned my lesson.

When I was first able to use the phone without my mom standing next to me for every conversation, I knew immediately of the power of a phone call. One day, there was a window of opportunity to make a call to Church Street. The house was empty. I made sure that the back door of our house that entered our kitchen was locked, and I made every precaution to ensure that I had my privacy.

I dialed her number. She answered. I immediately hung up.

I dialed her number again. She answered. I immediately hung up the phone again. This was the beginning of a trend that happened many times throughout my elementary years. While I was brave enough to "make" the call, I was not confident enough to carry on a conversation.

I waited a whole five more minutes to call again. Same result.

But I heard her voice and for some reason that was good enough for me. I had connected with her, even though she really had no clue who it was. It was my secret and I was the only one that ever knew it.

For the next year or so, every now and then, I would make this same phone call. It would always end the same way. Sometimes she would hang up. Sometimes there were long periods of silence before one of us would hang up.

One day my sister came into the kitchen and she was talking to her friend Lenora. They were talking loud and I did not hang up the phone soon enough; I was sure that Church Street had heard, and I would be exposed as the culprit of the constant phone calls. I was scared that she or her parents would call back and I would be in trouble. A call never came. I stopped making those phone calls.

Unfortunately, I have one memorable personal experience that involved Church Street, and this time she knew I was involved.

One school year, as Valentine's Day approached, I was already dreading the day when Valentine cards would be distributed in class. My mom had already bought the kind that were full of silly puns like: "You're swell" or "I like Bee-ing Your Friend" with a bee pictured on the card. All of them wishing the other person a Happy Valentine's Day. Usually, the cards were so generic that you could give them to any boy or girl without much thought. But there was never enough of them to cover the whole class, so I would sit at the kitchen table trying to select the right card for each classmate. You put them in piles. One pile for the boys in the class, another for the girls. However, trying to pick out the card to give to the girl you secretly "liked" was like trying to figure out the equation of nuclear fusion. You wanted to find the perfect card, not too forward but something that left no doubt of your interest.

That year, I was convinced that I only had cards for the girls. I struggled to find cards to give to the boys and it was even harder to find appropriate cards for the girls. I did not want to send the wrong message to a girl. It's my duty to say that a big part of my reluctance to giving such cards was my dread of the ridicule and teasing I might receive from having given cards to girls that might read into the note on the card. Anyway, there was that fear of ridicule which went beyond the already strong desire not to be the odd boy with a stuttering problem. I dreaded hearing that one boy, who would love to embarrass me, say to the class "Hey look! David gave a card with 'I like you' on it to _____!" My solution was to only give cards out to the boys. Safe, generic and no fear of ridicule cards. My mother, on the other hand, made sure that I made one out to every class member.

So, there I sat at the kitchen table, filtering each card and trying come up with a viable solution to my fears. My mom had somehow arrived at the notion that I should give every girl in the class (not to hurt any of their feelings for having been left out, always one of her prime concerns) a Valentine card. I don't know how my mother could have been so out of touch with the reality of elementary grade school life as to think that was something for a boy to do. The charm of the idea was so great for her that she would not yield to my objections, and I had to accept this unfortunate whim of hers.

The fateful day of our class Valentine party arrived. Full of dread, I dutifully took my cards to school and inserted them into the slots of our homemade Valentine boxes. The absurd thing about this Valentine card episode is that, despite my struggle against having to give cards to the girls, I had begun to hope that it might turn out to be a blessing in disguise regarding Church Street. Here was the opportunity, though one I would never have chosen, to let her subtlety know my interest in her. Certainly, her card was chosen carefully. It was the one I had truly taken care of, while striving to make it special. Surely hers was the one for which the words in some sense spoke the truth. I had no doubt that the card was beautiful. How could she not be struck by that beauty?

What a thrill it would be if she looked over at me and smiled with pleasure after admiring my card! I could picture her complimenting me on it as she thanked me for having given it to her. Perhaps my card would so impress her that its message would be met with favor. Perhaps she would even start to "like" me. What a boost it would be to my status in the class when her new fondness for me became known!

I watched intently as she went through the pile of Valentine cards on her desk, casually examining each one. Anxiety, anticipation, and hope mounted in me as she came to mine—and instantly she set it aside! She discarded my card with scarcely a glance! It was hand-picked just for her and she treated it as unworthy of a second's contemplation. It just was a trivial message from an insignificant boy.

Now to be fair… she never stopped and read one card more than the other. They were all met with the same reaction. It was just that card was mine and I had so much hope that she would acknowledge it with a smile or a head nod.

I don't know whether she had been aware that I was watching.

There was no look my way. I'm sure she never gave it a second thought or had any idea of the feeling of rejection her indifference had caused. But to me, it was a rejection, and nothing is worse for a man's ego than being rejected by a woman, even when the "man" and "woman" in question are only eleven-years-old.

Nothing had really changed, no one was any wiser to the event, except for the split second it took to dash my unwarranted hopes. The acid of disappointment became so concentrated that it etched the memory deep in my mind. The memory of Church Street's indifference to my carefully chosen card and its hidden message of "like" is still there, lurking in the back confines of my mind.

As I grew older, she and I would indeed talk. I am sure she knew of my interest and "liking" her but we never brought the subject up. We would talk when we would walk home from school and sometimes on the phone. I stopped making the "no talk" phone calls and if she had any clue it was me who was making those calls, she never indicated that she knew.

Now... I would like to point out that Church Street and I did "go out" one time. My family took her and I to the movies. "The Poseidon Adventure" was playing at the theatre in Port Clinton and I asked if she wanted to go and she did. Nothing like a disaster movie of a ship capsizing with mass casualties to set the mood for a successful romantic date.

In the coming years, Church Street and I would drift in different directions and eventually we stopped talking. I would find "love" the moment I laid eyes on the girl who would one-day become my wife.

I have no idea where Church Street is today, but I am grateful for these memories that are strong enough to place me back in my elementary years.

But this truth remains... I will never confirm, nor deny that she was my first kiss.

A gentleman never tells.

8

THE SONG REMEMBERS WHEN

I've been dabbling in writing my entire life. I have handwritten on 3-hole loose leaf notebook paper as far back as I can remember. It was a wonderful outlet to express my thoughts. No one would ever read my words and it was liberating.

Growing up, writing was just something I had to do. I hid it so well and no one really was aware of it. I wrote most of the stories that are found in this book many different times as I grew up. Each one would improve as I matured in my writing. As I shared earlier, life happened and at some point in my early 20's I buried all of those hand-written pages. I put them in a place where they will never be found. There is a part of me that regrets tossing them aside so easily, but I cannot change what I did and they will remain where they are today. I stopped writing and my stories and thoughts faded off into the void in my head where memories go to be forgotten. It was disappointing.

Years later, when the computer came along, I found a renewed passion for writing. The computer allowed for a place where I could write and "save" my writings and not have to worry about anyone reading my feelings and thoughts that I would write about. I wrote about random things, jobs, experiences, Christianity, faith, friends, hope, heartbreak, happiness, marriage, children, divorce, personal challenges, triumphs and frustrations. It was wonderful.

But then I started having flashes of memories and stories of growing up in a small town and I remembered that there was once a time that I had put many of these stories down on paper. What remained in my memory was still buried there, but I had to find a way to get them out once again. How could I do it? I wanted to write these stories out so that my family would know them long after I was no longer here. It was frustrating.

My challenge was to figure out a way to write these stories so that I could share not only the details of the story but my thoughts and feelings as I experienced the story once again. I sat down at the computer and tried to write. What that resulted in was a list of bullet points. Like Joe Friday from the old television show Dragnet, I was just regurgitating the facts. No emotion, no nostalgia and no connection to them. It was horrible.

I wanted the reader to be part of my journey and part of the story. I wanted them to experience the feelings as I did, even if those feelings were negative or sad. I needed to find a way to pull in the emotion that I was feeling in my heart and not just the facts of the story. For me, dealing with the emotional side of these stories was a healing process for me. I have carried the burden of these feelings and emotions in the confines of heart and my head for years. I spent many nights staring at an empty screen with no progress. I was discouraged and believed that the stories of my youth would forever remain buried with those loose-leaf notebooks. I was going to give up. It was depressing.

One morning, about 2:00 AM, I was staring at the blank screen glowing in the darkness and I put my headphones on. I couldn't sleep, and I was going to listen to music until I would grow tired and go to back to bed. I had to go to work in the morning.

With music streaming in my headphones, I sat there and at some point, the song, "I'll Play for You" by the band, Seals and Crofts came on. As the song starts, I feel the warmth of my youth sweep over me. Details of a story became clear and emotions overtake me. Tears fill my eyes and suddenly I am taken back to a memorable moment in my life. I remember thinking, "Wow... I forgot about that moment." It was perfect.

I opened my computer and placed my fingers on the keyboard. I thought, "Well, let me start thinking about where that happened and how I felt." The song helped me to relive the memory. The song remembered when I couldn't. Memories I'd long forgotten were now unearthed and the words just poured out of me.

That is what music does for me, it helps me remember the special moments as well as the difficult ones. The years pass and the details fade, but a couple of bars from one of the songs from my youth takes me back to a forgotten time, place and feeling. It was healing.

I was obsessed with getting these stories written and I think my wife was sure I was losing it. She would walk by and see me with tears in my eyes as I was frantically typing away on the keyboard. I would look up, smile, tell her that I was ok, and I would continue to write. I am not sure I ever convinced her though. For her, it was scary.

I made a personal commitment to write these stories again. I intended for them to be placed on a portable thumb drive that I would place in a safe in my house. I never planned on having them read by anyone else. My plan was for them to be discovered one day and maybe they would be something that my family would enjoy reading in the future. I had always wished that I could have a copy of the stories that my grandfather shared so that I could read them every now and then. That was my plan for these stories.

Lord knows I never planned on writing a book. The world doesn't need another rank amateur thinking they can write a book. However, I posted a few excerpts of a story about my brother Bobby on Facebook and suddenly I was having people contact me asking if they could read more. I gave a few stories to some friends to read and they all talked me into this project.

For the record, not one word of this book was written without music streaming in the background. I need to say that I have wondered why a certain song may bring back memories of a story that doesn't have anything to do with the song. For example, when the song, "Down on the Corner" by Creedence Clearwater Revival plays I am reminded of the bridge that covers the Portage River. I immediately remember the times that I went fishing at a spot just below the bridge. Great memory of a lot of fun but not many memories of catching fish. It wasn't about how many fish you caught, it was more about hanging out with your buddies. The song doesn't have a tie to the memory but every time I hear it this is where it takes me.

"In the year 2525" by the group Zager & Evans always reminds me of riding my bike around the old Griest Motor Sales building and looking at the permanent marker line that showed the highwater mark from the flood that hit Oak Harbor on July 4th, 1969. Why does this song evoke this memory? I don't have a clue.

The truth is... most of the significant events in my life have been marked by music. There are so many songs that remind me of people, places and special times in my life. For whatever reason, I have always associated different times in my life with the music I listened to. For example, my "first" favorite song that I really remember as a child was the 1967 release called, "The Rain, the Park & Other Things" by the Cowsills. Being 6 or 7 at the time, I only knew it as the "Flower Girl" song. To this very day, when I hear this song I am transported back to another place and another time. I can smell the dinner that my mom is fixing in the kitchen and I clearly remember sitting on my bed with a transistor radio in my hand desperately trying find a station that would play my song.

I remember in early 1973, long before they became the rock icons they are today, my best friend Bryan came to school sporting a tee-shirt with the name "Aerosmith" blazing across the front. Today, all I have to hear is a song by them and in my mind, Bryan and I are hanging out in his basement. Just like the basement from "That 70's Show". I won't tell you what character best represents me and NO!! it isn't Donna or Jackie. Let's just say that I can relate to the whole show and the dynamics of friendship and having a community basement to hang out in.

When I hear a song from Elton John, especially songs from an album called "Blue Moves," I am reminded of Kim Hutchison and the wonderful times I had with her and her family. She gave me that album for Christmas and I hold those memories close to my heart. They were fun days, filled with ice skating, going to church and just hanging out. It was truly one of the most carefree times in my life.

All I have to hear is the first note to "My Girl" by The

Temptations and I am completely overcome with thoughts and memories of the first moment I met the girl who would one day become my wife. Pam has been and will remain "home" for me.

These are just a few examples of what goes through my mind when I hear the songs from that period of my life. Not every song brings about such memories, but those that do allow me to see things in color.

Because even if I have forgotten, the song remembers when.

9

BEEN THERE, DONE THAT

On a recent drive through my small town, I drove past the house we lived in on Locust Street. I drove slowly to take a good look at the porch where snow had drifted completely over it by the blizzard that covered Northwest Ohio 1978. The night before the blizzard, I remember playing street football with the Haley boys and the other neighborhood kids on the familiar Oak Street "field".

This day I turn onto Oak Street and I stop in the familiar spot where I parked my car for years. Like most things you see after being gone for a long period of time, I notice how small that area is. In my memory it was much bigger, but I will say that it still looks exactly as I remember it. Sure, the houses and trees are older now, but so am I and for the most part it is exactly as my memory holds it.

I continued to drive down Locust Street and I pass the area at the east end of Walnut Street to a place that led to what we called the "Stockyard Pond". I am not sure that it is even there anymore. Maybe it has been filled in and now is just a field where once a pond had been. But I have the distinct memory of being there with my brother Bobby as he tried to catch something he called a "dog fish."

I remember that the more he talked about this fish, the more it scared me. I am sure he was embellishing the story or making it up because he could see the fear in my eyes. I never saw him catch this mystery fish, but he convinced me it was in that pond. I have no idea if it was real or if anyone ever caught it. In my heart, if it was real, I hope it lived a long and prosperous life and that it stayed a mystery to all.

As I drive north on Locust Street, I turn left onto South Railroad Street. I am reminded of how many times my mom told me I was not allowed to cross the tracks that ran just north of the street. I would cross them many times without her knowledge to play football or to hang out with the kids that lived on the other side of those tracks. I have great memories of epic football games played on cold fall days.

I can't help but to reminisce about the kids that played in these games. Today, kids don't seem to do that anymore. Back then it was what we did every day. Our dreams of becoming a professional baseball or football player had not yet been dashed upon the rocks of reality. We believed they could come true for all of us. We could, in fact, all play professionally and we all would play on the same team. Like the pick-up games in our backyard, we were only limited by what we dreamed. I have no idea whatever happened to those group of kids.

During the summer, our day was marked by a bike race to Van Atta's Dairy Queen to get our .15 ice cream cone. Then we would make the mad dash home to play baseball until we would get too hot to play and then, if we did not have a game that night, we would make our daily trip to the pool.

We never swam on game days. We were told we couldn't because it would make us too tired and we would not be able to play at the top of our game. We were convinced that the lifeguards were going to call our coaches.

On game days, we would ride our bikes to the pool; not only just to see the girls but to see the fun we were missing with our other friends that did not have a game. We would stare through the fence for a while then slowly head home one-by-one to rest up for the game. Baseball was life during that time. We never considered that there had never been one player in our small town that ever made it. For now, our dreams were safely protected by the belief of the certainty of the young and naive.

I could write a book about Teagarden's pool. Let's just say I have so many life experiences and events that surround my time there. The pool was about a three-minute bike ride from our home on Walnut Street. At the young age of 7, I was trusted to go there by myself and generally stay away from my mother's oversight.

In today's world, parents must escort their children everywhere. A 7-year-old waiting in line to get in to swim unattended by a parent or at least an older brother or sister would be eyed with some suspicion. But that is the way it was back in those days.

I don't have to strain to remember the strong smell of chlorine that came from the small building that housed the restrooms. This wonderful place is where I finally learned that girls weren't so horrible after all. I have clear memories of always finding a reason to strategically position myself in the water along the side of the pool so I had a clear view of the girls sunbathing at the north end of the building.

On this day, I turn onto Jefferson Street and try to remember exactly where the parking lot and pool were located. The pool was filled in with dirt and the building next to the pool was torn down years ago. I see no evidence of the building nor of the pool. No one would believe that a pool was once located there. This glorious space on this street held so many memories for so many people.

I stop my car where I believe the pool was once located and I immediately remember something that Bryan and I did on one of those nights I stayed over at his house. We snuck out of his house about 1:00 AM and walked our way down to the pool. We decided that it would be a great idea to climb the fence and do a little swimming.

We had heard rumors that this was something some older kids had done. We really thought we were doing something daring and dangerous. We made our way towards the pool and we were starting our way across the parking lot when we see the headlights of a car that turned onto Jefferson Street. Immediately, Bryan and I run to hide behind some bushes and we watch the Oak Harbor Police shine their light through the fence of the pool. Suddenly the police car stops and pulls in the parking lot of the pool and the officer gets out of the car and starts yelling for the kids who were hiding in the pool to get out and come over to him at the fence.

We couldn't believe it. There were older kids already in the pool and they got caught. We watched as the officer made them climb over the fence and get in the back of the police car. We didn't move. We feared getting caught. So, we stayed quiet and remained still until the police left. We lost our nerve and made our way back to his house. When we would tell stories and lies to our other friends, we always said we climbed the fence and went swimming... but the truth is we chickened out.

I turn my car around and make my way up Church Street and I turn right onto Washington Street. I pulled my car over next to the old football stadium and park on the side of the road, just before the railroad tracks. Suddenly, I remember the haze from the stadium lights that used to float like a cloud all over the town. The familiar bleachers and the concession stands are now all gone. The high school doesn't play their games at this field anymore.

I found myself walking along the railroad tracks to look at what was left of the stadium that brought about so many memories for me. I notice there is little evidence of the black cinder track that once circled the football field. It now looks like the cinders were replaced by white stones.

Looking east onto that field, in my memory, I can still see the bleachers as they were in the early 70's. I remember how bright the Friday night lights were and I could smell the popcorn from the concession stands. We would watch the game from our perch on the railroad tracks. Not often, but every now and then a train would make its way through town during a game. We would all wait until halftime to go into the stadium for free.

On those Friday nights it always seemed like what happened on that field was the center of the whole world. When the crowd cheered, you could hear it all over town.

I now look down at the field where in my mind legends played. I am aware that these same legends are now grandparents, retired from their careers and living in the confines of the same town limits they swore they would leave as soon as high school was over.

I looked at the goal line at the end zone. The line is now faded and there doesn't seem to be much football played on that hallowed ground anymore. Looking at that washed-out goal line, I now realize that sometimes on Friday nights the home team won, sometimes they lost. It seemed of high significance at the time, but I would soon realize that the goal line was not important at all. In the coming years, I would come to realize that there were endless goal lines that I would have to face in life. Most of them were not of my own choosing. One goal line would appear in my life and once I reached it, it would disappear, only to be replaced by another one off in the distance.

I get back into my car and I make my way back to my old neighborhood on Walnut Street once again. I am trying to drive slowly, but not too slow so that anyone would think I am stalking or casing the block. As I drive up the street, I hear this "THWACK" sound, then silence. Then another thwack sound. And again.

A kid was throwing a tennis ball up against the side of his garage. It hit the garage and then bounced back onto the driveway: he caught it, paused, then threw it again.

I smiled, and I remember doing this exact same thing as a young boy. I hadn't seen a kid do this in years. When growing up, my own boys did not do it. We played a lot of wiffleball, but never once did I ever see my kids play with a tennis ball like I did as a child.

I guess I never thought about it much and considered it something that kids didn't do these days. Now all these years later, I see a boy doing what I spent hours doing during the summer.

I had this feeling sweep over me and I could not help but think that this young boy had taken my place in the neighborhood.

I stop my car to take a closer look at what the boy was doing. I cannot tell what a joy it was to see this boy's expression. There was an excitement and determination in this boy's face. I could see his lips moving as he was doing full color commentating. He was doing a play-by-play for the audience he pretended was there. Much like I did when I was young, he was pretending to be someone else. Someone who was a hero to him. Maybe he was pretending to be a baseball player, or maybe a football player. There was no way to tell. The imagination of this boy was running at full force and his imagination could allow a tennis ball to become whatever he wanted it to be.

In his mind, his driveway had become a big-time arena. The tennis ball thwacked against the garage once more. It bounced back to him and he caught it. He once again made a game saving play in some stadium somewhere in his imagination. Physically he was safe by the confines of his home, but his mind and heart were a long way off in the distance.

Not a bad combination.

I know. I've been there and done just that.

10

SOME CALLS CHANGE YOUR LIFE

I had no intention of driving to Oak Harbor that day. I left work and for some reason, I turned east on State Route 163. Something was drawing me to drive past our house on Walnut Street. Maybe it was trying to reconnect with my childhood or maybe it was just simple curiosity, but something was drawing me back to drive past our old house.

So, as I passed Kozy Korners restaurant, I make the hard-left turn onto Benton Street.

I am driving really slow so that I can take in the sites and make sure I don't miss anything. I wanted to look and see if it was the same as my memory convinced me that it was. The houses seem so much smaller to me. I had to remind myself that my memories are filtered through the eyes of a nine-year-old boy. Everything seemed bigger to me in 1970.

I pass Toussaint Street and I slowly drive past the spot where I crashed my bike and broke my right arm when I was ten. It looks just like it did back then. I then make a right-hand turn onto Walnut Street. I pass Burdine's old house on the corner and suddenly I am taken back in time. For the most part, the houses look the same. The names of those living in those homes, however, I'm sure have long since changed.

The street lights were starting to turn on and there wasn't any movement on the block. No traffic, no kids playing in the street or in their front yards. There was just silence. Apart from a few lights that shined through the windows, it was as if the neighborhood just froze in time and knew I was coming to visit. Through the trees that lined Walnut Street, I saw the slant of rain falling. The trees bowed low and hung in a welcoming gesture. I was back to where the roots of my childhood were planted.

I stopped the car in the middle of the street and looked up at the window of the bedroom that I shared with my brother Bobby and wondered if it still looked the same. As I stare into that old bedroom window on the second floor, I am flooded with the memory of taping a cardboard box to the back of the closet door. We used a lot of tape to secure it to the door. We needed a lot of tape to make sure that it stayed up because it always got a lot of use. We cut the bottom out of the box so that anything you dropped through the top would go right through. That was the point. My brother and I would roll up a pair of socks and play bedroom basketball.

My brother Bobby was never much of a sports guy. But this was something we would do together. At some point during the day, usually at night and just before we would go to bed, this is what we would do. We would feint and lunge, and we would try to fool each other with our moves. We would put our backs to the basket and try hook shots with these balled up rolls of socks. It would always end up with one of us trying the impossible shot that would only be blind luck if it went through the basket. But we sure would crow and act like it was all skill. In our minds, luck had nothing to do with it.

We would always start playing with the intent of trying to make it as real as possible, but eventually, it was just my brother trying to one-up me and taking advantage of his size to beat me. It would end up with each of us throwing balled up socks at each other in anger which would then result in him bowling me over, or hitting me because I may have "scored a basket" on him. Either way, I was usually the one that would end up crying and hurt. My mom would have to intervene and make sure I was ok and yell at us to "quiet down" or she would have to get out the broom.

Now let me tell you about the broom closet.

My mom was a stay-at-home homemaker. She raised us. My dad was a truck driver and was only home on the weekends. My mother ruled with an iron fist. She had to. Being under 5' tall she always needed an equalizer. That equalizer was the broom. Or to be clearer, the broom "stick." Now, I must admit that I have never witnessed my mother ever using the broom "stick" on any of us. In fact, while I am sure she did, I don't have any recollection of her ever raising a hand towards me. But back then, the mere mention of the broom would get our attention right away. There are very few things that I fear in life, but I will tell you, to this very day, I still have extreme respect and an element of fear when it comes to my mom threatening to get the broom out. My mom is the only human I ever knew that grew to 10-foot tall and became bullet-proof when she was mad. We knew not to press our luck when she jiggled the handle of the broom closet.

Each night we would work up a sweat, showing off and bragging and like always, it would wind up being a brawl. Mom would intervene, and we always seemed to settle our differences then the next night we would be back at it with the same result.

Looking back, I loved those games. We'd keep score. I still remember the laughter, the shouts of triumph and victory that filled that room. Those sounds far outweigh any memories of the fights that would happen. Those memories are very precious to me.

From my car, I look at the rain-streaked window of that bedroom. There was no light inside and it dawned on me that I have no idea who sleeps in that room at night and wakes each morning in a room that once was filled with brothers that really had nothing in common except for sharing a last name, a bedroom and a sock bedroom basketball game that we played together. I had no idea that it all would come to a screeching halt. There was no warning and no way to prepare for the events of that dark day.

As I sit in my car, staring at that bedroom window, I am overcome with emotion and I start to cry. I have passed this house hundreds of times over the years and I never broke down in tears before. On this day, however, I am reminded that after all these years, I still struggle with grief. I have heard other people say that grief comes in waves. My experience tells me that's not what I have experienced when it comes to grief.

What I have experienced since that cold brisk November day in 1970 are not waves of grief. To be honest, instead of feeling waves of grief that come every now and then, I personally have felt grief every single day. No waves, just one consistent shade of grey that washes over me. It is something that is part of me. It isn't something that I chose to have in my life and I work hard at hiding it, but it is always there. It has been my life-long companion and it is as normal in my life as putting my clothes on in the morning. To go about my day, I must put clothes on. I can never consider another option without striking fear and disgust from those who would see me naked and exposed. That is what grief is to me. Like the clothes I must wear, it is something that I put on every day. I don't have a choice. I wish I could, but I can't wash it off in the shower. I push it down inside of me as far as I can, but it's always lurking and hiding somewhere just under the surface. It is a grey filter that clouds my world and I have carried this dark passenger with me since I was nine.

What blindsides and attacks me when I least expect it, is not grief.

It's guilt.

I never talk about this with anyone. Not even with my wife. It is something that I have struggled with since that horrible day. Guilt comes to me in these huge sucker-punch hits that I never see coming. They hit me so hard that it rams into my very soul. It feels as if someone has hit you so hard in the stomach that it sucks out everything you have – your heart, your oxygen, your whole being. It hits me out of nowhere. I cannot predict when or where it will show up. I cannot control it.

The pangs of guilt hit me when I am doing some of the most mundane, common things in life. Like they hit when I am driving in my car to work, or when I am listening to music or working in my garage. There have been times when they have hit me when I shop at the grocery store. Of course, no one else knows it. I remain calm and stoic. I smile at the person I pass in the same aisle, and I continue filling my cart with milk and bread. But it's there, spasms of guilt, flooding my heart and my thoughts. A sucker-punch of the worst kind. No one is the wiser and I carry on with life. Never knowing when it will run into me next. Never knowing when I will be so overcome with guilt that I cannot even speak.

I sort of live in fear of that.

However, lately, the pangs of guilt are most evident when I walk into a room and glance up and see the pictures of my wife, children, and grandchildren. I see the pictures hung on the walls of my home. All of them depicting family. Each one representing a moment in time. The smiles, frozen in time, that tell a story of a life lived and enjoyed. Lives that are filled with potential and a future.

While we are never guaranteed to live long on this earth, my children and grandchildren, for the most part, have been spared of the loss and heartache that comes from someone in their life taken way too soon. For that I am grateful, but for all of us, it soon will be inevitable. They each will experience loss and they must deal with the dark passenger of grief that comes with the loss of a loved one. My prayer is that they will not have to endure the guilt, as I have, that can sometimes be associated with such loss.

Guilt. My enemy. My nemesis. As much as it hits me at random times, there is never a time that I am barraged more with it than when I write. Every time… and always.

When I write I can express my thoughts and my feelings. It honestly is how I have learned to cope with the grief and guilt that I carry in my life. Probably it is why when I write, I usually tell stories of something bad or embarrassing happening to me. Writing about the things that have been difficult or disparaging makes the guilt dissipate for me. It dissolves the blame that I feel and it allows me to process it into something that gives me perspective and helps me know my place in life.

For the record, I am keenly aware of the great things that have happened to me in my life. I have traveled around the world and spent extended times in Africa and South America. I have met two US presidents, swam in the Amazon River and have sojourned the plains of Africa on safari to see the wonder of God's creation. I worked for a long period of my life doing exactly what God put me on this earth to do. I eventually married my soul mate and the love of my life. I was there for the birth of my children and have watched each of them grow into successful adults that contribute to the world in a better way. These things point to a life that has been successful and one worth living. Considering my background and where I came from, these events were so improbable, so unexpected, that even today when I think of these things, I tend to believe they happened to another person or they didn't happen at all. However, they did happen to me. They are stories to be told another time, but even though these are great experiences, they have just left another layer of guilt that I have had to come to terms with.

I know I am not alone in dealing with these types of things and I am sure that everyone can relate to the grief that life gives. But why the guilt? Not everyone lives their life beset with guilt. I don't know why I have never been able to shake the pangs of guilt that fill my heart and mind. I have tried so hard to suppress them over the years. The results have manifested themselves into other issues that have made life difficult for me at times. Even though I do not in any way use it as an excuse, I know that my guilt has manifested itself into being a very angry young man. This anger has resulted in me having a very short temper. This temper has gotten the best of me more than I care to be reminded. My family, especially my wife and children, all have experienced me "losing" my temper for reasons that they do not understand. Many times, it happens over the simplest and everyday issues. The end result would just add to the burden of guilt that I carry. I am not the same man I was twenty years ago when it comes to my temper, but that anger, and guilt, is still there, and I pray daily that I keep it in check.

I have nothing else to say other than this. I was nine when my brother died. There is no other way to say it. It is a simple statement yet defining. In full disclosure, I was not emotionally equipped to handle this type of trauma. But then again who is? My vulnerability has deep roots into in my childhood. I have always been protected from the outside world by my mom. After all, I was the baby of the family and I have always been treated accordingly.

If you considered my world in 1970, you would have found that other than the 6:30 news bringing the horrors of the Vietnam War, the Manson Murders and the Kent State shootings into our living room, I was protected from the outside world. The bad news that was projected on our black and white television was often tempered by shows like Bonanza, Mayberry RFD, the Beverly Hillbillies and Gilligan's Island. This was long before reality TV. Almost all the programs on our television at the time were based on some type of non-reality life. The premise of a hillbilly living in Hollywood with a cement pond, or the reality of a group of people, on a three-hour tour, to be forever stranded on a deserted island was all the reality we needed.

The real issues and aspects of life were confined to a half hour of news. Everything else was filtered by the security of living in a place that was doing everything it could to keep the real world from crossing the town limit signs.

Sunday nights were always the best time of the week for me. I don't know why, other than the fact that some of my favorite TV shows came on that night. I remember sitting around the TV watching Mutual of Omaha's Wild Kingdom. It was amazing how Marlin Perkins watched, while Jim Fowler did all the work. Even at nine-years-old, I sat at the edge of my seat, noticing how the host, Marlin, would be calm, cool and collected when his sidekick, Jim, would be in grave danger because of the wild beast they were pursuing that evening. The suspense would build but before the show ended, like always, it would work out and we would have to tune in next week to see another thrilling adventure. It was one of my favorite shows growing up.

Watching the Wonderful World of Disney and the Ed Sullivan Show would cap off my Sunday night and I would have to be forced to go to bed. I was in the 4th grade and even though I got to stay up later than my brothers and sister did when they were my age, I still had to be in bed for a good night's sleep.

In early October 1970, I had some medical issues that required surgery. I was being admitted into Magruder Hospital in Port Clinton, Ohio. I was going to have surgery and I would be absent for two-weeks from Mrs. Gulau's classroom at R.C. Water's Elementary School.

Mrs. Gulau was my 4th-grade teacher. While there is no doubt that she was a wonderful teacher, she seemed ancient to me. She seemed out of touch even by Oak Harbor standards. Mrs. Gulau was old school before old school was a thing. She was a strict teacher. She allowed no excuses for missing homework assignments and ran her classroom like a well-oiled machine. No deviation from the schedule was permitted. I struggled with her being my teacher and I will admit it wasn't her fault.

It was mine.

At the young age of nine, I had figured out that the best way to get through school was to not make waves. At all costs, I would try to not get noticed and for the love of all things pure and holy, I never raised my hand to answer a question. I was always smarter than I ever let on, but I wasn't willing to try and talk in front of people for fear of my stuttering and making myself look foolish in front of people. I was content to fade into the background. I was easy to not remember. I am sure if you asked a few of my classmates from that school year, they would struggle to remember me.

Just someone they used to know.

After a few days in the hospital, I was discharged. I was homebound for a week before I was permitted to go back to school. After I started going back to class, Mrs. Gulau had made a schedule with my mother to have me stay after school for a few weeks to catch up on my studies. I would stay until 3:45 PM, about an hour after school let out for the rest of the students.

Then November 5th, 1970 happened.

It was a cool day, about 45 degrees and a little windy as I remember it. I had a pretty good day at school and I was finally feeling like I was getting back into the routine of Mrs. Gulau's classroom. The school day ended, and I completed my hour of tutoring with my teacher. I was now waiting by the west side door that the teachers used. Normally, I always came in and left through the front door of the school. I always rode the bus that would take me and the kids from my neighborhood to the high school on Church Street. From there, we would meander the two blocks or so to get home in time to watch Gilligan's Island that came on at 4:00 PM every day after school.

But the last few days were different. There wasn't a late bus to take me home and I was too young to walk all that way back home before it got dark at 5:30 PM. So, I stood there in silence as Mrs. Gulau looked impatiently out the door to see if my ride was there yet. My cousin, Larry, was picking me up and he was obviously running a little late.

I always heard Larry's car before I could ever see it. Not because his car ran bad or had a loud exhaust system, but rather Larry always played his music loud. I mean loud. As predicted, Larry's music was blaring from his car as he pulled up to the side door to pick me up.

Larry turned down the music and the passenger side door flew open as he stopped the car. I mumbled, "Goodbye," to Mrs. Gulau and I saw the look on her face as she pushed the school door open as I started out to get into the car. I wasn't sure if it was because of the loud music or because he was late to pick me up. Either way, it was clearly a look of displeasure that she was giving.

Larry said, "What's her problem?" as I slid into the front passenger seat of his Chevy Corvair. I responded, "I have no idea." and then I hear my brother Bobby and his best friend, Buster laughing from the back seat. They were always laughing when they were together. I never really knew what they laughed about all the time but here they were laughing about something and they were the only ones that knew why. Buster was the son of my mom's best friend, Leta Chandler. It made perfect sense for Bobby and him to be best friends.

I slam the car door closed and Larry cranks the music even louder than before just to see if he can get another reaction from the teacher. She disappears into the darkened hallway, shaking her head with displeasure, and we pull out onto Ottawa Street to head back to our house on Walnut Street.

I settle into my seat and I notice that my brother's dog was with him. "What are you guys doing?" I ask.

"Wouldn't you like to know!!" my brother quipped in sarcasm, as only brothers can. It was as if he knew I was going to ask that question. Buster and Bobby mumble something to each other and they burst out laughing again.

Larry, seeing that my feelings were going to get hurt by the banter that happens organically between brothers, put his cigarette down and said, "I'm dropping them off so they can check their traps on Mylander's farm."

"Can I go with you?" I asked inquisitively.

"Dude, your mom told me to bring you straight home. You're

going to have to ask her. But you're going to have to ask fast because I have to get to work soon." Larry replied.

I nodded in silence and I distinctly remember the song, "Lola" by the Kinks was blaring on the radio. My brother and Buster were laughing and playing with the dog in the backseat. I was right where I loved to be. I always rode around town with Larry whenever I could. I loved it because Larry would play the music loud and he would tell me stuff about why this song was great and why he felt that song wasn't good. I always felt accepted and thought he enjoyed having me around.

Larry and I had a bond that was different than the one I had with my oldest brother Jim. Jim always seemed way older than Larry. I always felt like I was just a nuisance to Jim. I was his irritating little brother. I was always in the way. He was a senior, and his interests were on his girlfriend, sports, and his future. In that order. He really didn't have a lot of time to spend with his little brother. Life and all its responsibilities were in front of him. His future was uncertain. With the Vietnam War raging on the other side of the world and the military draft being active, he had no idea where he was going to end up. College wasn't an option, so he would have to roll the dice and see what was going to happen. So, he did what older brothers have been doing since the beginning of time. He ignored me. Larry too was a senior, but he never treated me that way. Even though I was only nine, he made me feel like we were friends more than just cousins.

Besides the occasional outburst of laughter that came from my brother and Buster from the back seat, we rode back to our house in silence. Only the sounds of the Kink's reverberating throughout the car.

We pull into the driveway and I see my mom waiting by the kitchen screen door. She was obviously wondering where we were because we were getting back a little later than normal. Larry turned down the radio and as the car comes to a stop, I push the car door open and step up on the seat of the car and pull myself up to look over the roof.

"Hey, Ma, can I ride with Larry to drop Bobby off?" I asked.

"No, Larry is running late and dinner will be ready soon" she responded.

"Come on Ma! Larry said he would drop me back off" I yelled.

"I said NO!!" she pushed back. "Come on in the house so Larry can get to work."

I started to respond but the backrest of the car seat flew forward and my brother started to climb out from the back seat. As he pushes me away from the car he says, "Come on Larry, let's go before it gets too dark".

I am so angry that my mom would not let me go. I had been working so hard after school to get caught up in my schoolwork, that I could not believe that she wouldn't let me do this one thing. I mean, I hadn't been able to ride around with Larry for a long time and this seemed like the perfect opportunity to me. I trudged over to the front door and my mom opened the door a little wider to let me in. I stormed past her, bumping her with my shoulder. I hit her hard enough that I was certain she was going to grab my arm and make me settle down, but she didn't.

I stormed through the kitchen and down the hallway to the living room. All the while, mumbling under my breath about how unfair it was and how angry I was with my mom for not letting me go with them.

My sister, Linda, was already in the living room watching TV and an episode of Gilligan's Island had already started. I heard the radio from Larry's car as he pulled out of the driveway and headed down to Benton Street. I sat myself angrily down on the couch and pulled the curtain back and watched that black Corvair disappear on its way down the street. I turned around and started to watch the TV.

It seemed like only a few seconds before I started to hear the shrill whine of the sirens. We lived a few blocks from the main siren in town, but for some reason, it seemed unusually loud and never-ending.

My mom walks into the living room and doesn't say a word, but just the look on her face tells me that something is wrong. No words are spoken, and she makes her way down the hall and disappears back into the kitchen. It is then the kitchen door bursts open and I hear unfamiliar voices coming from the kitchen and in an instant, there is chaos in our house. I hear a voice above the noise, "There has been an accident and they think it's the Lee boys!!"

I hear my mom talking but I can't make out what she is saying, and my sister and I are left alone in the living room just staring at each other trying to process the chaos that has just forced its way into our lives.

Next thing I know, Linda and I are shuttled upstairs into my parent's bedroom and we were told that our mom was going to check on our brother. Nothing else was said to us and the door was closed to separate us from the rest of the house. We sat on the edge of my parent's bed, knowing that something bad happened but we did not know what it was. We never considered that death was a possibility. Our family had only dealt with the death of a great-grandmother and none of us had ever considered that it would touch our family.

With my sister and me quietly sequestered upstairs in my parent's bedroom, there wasn't much need to check in on us. We could hear the commotion downstairs. The loudness, the overlapping voices, the sudden periods of extreme quietness. The constant opening and closing of our back door.

Finally, I had enough. I snuck out my parent's bedroom door and made my way quietly down the wooden steps of our home. The landing of the stairwell opened into our living room and it was filled with people. People that I am sure were familiar to me but as I recollect they all seemed faceless, except for their eyes. It seemed to me that people looked through me as if I did not exist. People who did not know what to say or simply ignored the traumatized nine-year-old that was walking in their midst. I made my way down the dark hallway towards our kitchen.

As I got to the doorway that leads into our kitchen, I heard my mom talking on the phone. It was at that moment that I would learn the truth. "I need to get a message to Robert Lee" my mom pleaded. "I need him to call home as soon as possible because his son was killed today in a car accident."

Some calls change your life forever.

All I could do was stand there. Blankly staring. Wondering if this was a dream or real-life. I finally knew the truth. But what did that really mean? What just happened?

After pulling out of our driveway, Larry's black Corvair made its way down Walnut Street and made a right turn onto Benton Street. With the music blaring as loud as the cheap speakers would allow, they made their way towards the railroad crossing at the town limit sign at the end of Benton Street. Buster in the backseat behind Larry as he drove and my brother sitting in the passenger seat with his back to the passenger door so that he could talk to Buster in the backseat.

The Penn-Central engineer that was operating the train stated that the car approached the train tracks and slowed to almost a complete stop. There were no crossing gates at this crossing and the engineer said he thought that he saw a woman in the passenger front seat with her back to the door. He said that he blew the train's whistle and that the car just slowly continued to cross the tracks after looking like it was going to stop. He saw no reaction in the car. No indication that Larry ever saw the train.

The train hit the car at over 70 MPH. They were killed instantly.

In his deposition, the engineer admitted that the speed limit at that portion of the tracks was 35 MPH. The train hit the car just behind the passenger side door. The car split in two. The front portion came to rest north of the tracks and the rear portion of the car was attached to the train's engine. It carried it for almost a mile before coming to a stop.

The days that followed were a blur.

The world seemed cold, vacant, strange.

The next thing I remember is standing in the middle of the funeral home with the stench of freshly cut flowers lingering in the air like an old lady's cheap perfume.

The boys were placed in closed caskets.

I didn't know it at the time, but the concept of having a closed casket would change my way of thinking. Regardless of what I was told by my family at that time, I am aware of the reasons they were all in closed caskets. I am thankful that I do not have memories of seeing them lying there. I was traumatized enough as it was. I did not need those images forever burned in my memory.

Today, I am comforted in knowing that my last memories of them are filtered images of them listening to music and hearing the banter, laughter and seeing the smiles on their faces. It was something that has helped me to move on from that difficult time. It has influenced me to the extent that when I die, I have requested to have a closed casket at my funeral. I understand that family will need some time to have some closure, but the truth is, the whole funeral process is for my family and not for me. I say put a picture of me of when I was young and skinny on top of the casket and let that image be the lasting image my grandchildren and family see.

Two days after the accident, the funeral home was filled with so many people. All three were at the same funeral home. The line to walk past each casket with each set of parents standing next them was long. It lined itself all through the funeral home and out the front door and down the sidewalk. Each person trying to figure out what to say to my mom and dad. Most of these people I probably knew, but again, to me, they were all faceless, except for their eyes. Eyes that seemed to be still staring, still watching and still observing our every move.

I grew up in an era before there were support groups. I grew up in a time that, if tragedy befell, you were pretty much on your own. Your family, whatever was left of it, was there. Your friends were there. But mostly you were the one who had to deal with the devastation yourself.

These well-meaning people were betrayed by their eyes. Their eyes told the story of the horror of losing a child, each trying to imagine what it must be like to lose a brother or a sister. Eyes that offered sympathetic looks but thankful that it wasn't them standing next to the casket of their child.

To say everyone was in shock is an understatement. Very few words were ever spoken by anyone. The roar of silence was so loud that it was hard to hear words when spoken. The awkward silence was deafening. It was hard for everyone. People didn't know what to say and those that could find words to say just came to say how sorry they were.

I am so glad that I had my friends. There are only a handful of people in your life who know you well enough to understand when the right thing to say is nothing at all. They know that the right thing to do is to sit there with you.

To be there.

Those people – and regardless of how lucky you are in your friendships, there will be, at most, only a few of them in your life. Those people will be with you in your very worst times. When you think that you cannot bear that which the world has hit you with, the silent presence of those friends will be all that you have, and that is all that matters.

I remember that the sun shone brightly through the thick beveled glass windows of the funeral home. It seemed so wrong. Dark clouds and rain would have been far more appropriate, but there wasn't a cloud in the sky. Each room filled with sunshine that highlighted the delicate, colorful flowers and plants that lined the walls and were staged neatly around each casket. These flowers and plants all sent by well-intentioned people, some to ease their guilt because they could not be there or for others, to show their sympathy for our loss. I must admit that the smell of flowers, to this very day, makes me feel sick to my stomach.

Today, I have a very clear and distinct memory of having an older brother. But the thing is, unless I see a picture, I can't remember what he looked like. I don't remember his voice. I remember him going to school every morning. I remember him teasing me. I remember our epic sock bedroom basketball games. I remember his friends he would have over and me begging him to let me play with them. I remember the color of his hair that was always messy. I remember a few days just before he was killed that we sat in his room playing "I'll Be There" by the Jackson 5 over and over until our mom yelled upstairs for us to turn it off. To this very day, I can't listen to that song without having tears stream down my face. I guess while some memories fade and details blur, some memories of a 9-year-old never quite leave you.

Waves of grief? No.

Guilt. Absolutely.

As an adult, I get the reasons why things happened the way they did that day. No one did anything intentional.

Everyone was in shock. No one ever spoke to me about it. In fairness, I never spoke a word about it either. No one sat down with me and helped me come to terms that it was just an accident. No one ever saw the guilt that was heaped onto my shoulders. No one saw that there was a nine-year-old boy who, to this very day, carries the weight for what happened.

Why did I have surgery that October? Why couldn't it have waited until Christmas break? Why did I have to stay after school? Why did I think I had to go with them? Why did I ask my mom in the first place? Surely my delay caused this to happen. Why didn't I protest more about not being able to go with Larry? Maybe I should have taken more time and delayed them. The train would have passed before they got to the railroad crossing. Thirty seconds either way and the results would have been so different.

Somewhere deep inside of me is still that young boy and he will never completely come to terms with the results of that day. The same could be said for my dad, mom, my brother and sister too. I am sure that they have their own grief and must deal with the guilt that comes from these kinds of tragedies.

We have never discussed this as a family.

Life should be lived, and you must move forward.

However, it doesn't lessen the pain of guilt that I experience. I feel guilty because I have been able to live a long life. I have been able to experience the wonderful things that this life has to offer.

My brother and my cousin Larry never got to experience the joy of bringing a child into this world. They didn't get to travel around the world or shake the hands of two U.S. presidents like I did.

They will never hear the joyous sound of a grandchild yelling, "Grandpa!!!" in excitement when you walk into a room and they see you.

After all these years, the pangs of guilt don't come as often, but they still lurk in the dark places and appear at the most unexpected times.

The heart of a nine-year-old was never made to process such things.

11

IN SIMPLE WORDS

*W*hat took place two days after my brother was killed has been such a huge part of my story; yet, while I do not intend to make this book about this event, I cannot deny it's importance, influence and impact on my life. It fundamentally changed my future and it has been the basis for which I have made decisions and for what I would do for the rest of my life.

The date was November 7, 1970.

When your brother dies unexpectedly and your life shatters like broken glass, everything is suddenly about your brother being dead. This means you don't know how to feel about doing the normal things you must do. I didn't know what the coming days' activities would entail. I was certain that I was doing the funeral process wrong. I was so sad, but also, I felt guilty that I wasn't sad about the right things, or sad about them in the right way.

People would cry when they saw my family. Me? I couldn't cry at that time. I was in shock and I had not processed the reality that just thrust itself onto our family. I probably have cried more over the last 10 years about the accident than I did at the funeral all those years ago.

I need to remind myself that there's no wrong way to grieve.

We lived in a small town where everyone knew my brother and

my cousin. People I never met were expressing condolences. I was edgy at the visitation because I was nervous that I would see someone I knew. I did not want to stare at them while they stared at me. I had no words to say. It was twisted, and I was cautious of being drawn into conversations I didn't want.

It was Saturday and we were well into the visitation portion of the funeral. Robinson's Funeral Home in Oak Harbor was filled with people. It was overwhelming for everyone. All three of the boys were at the same funeral home. Bobby and Larry on one side of the home and Harold "Buster" was on the other.

My Aunt Brenda had arrived at the funeral home and I was always so happy to see her. She and I always seemed to click when I was growing up. She spoke in a way that I could always understand, and she always listened and allowed me to ask questions. I was so glad to see her. When I was in the hospital for my surgery just weeks before the accident, she made me an embroidered pillow that I still have to this day. I always felt comforted and safe when she was around. It was awkward to smile and be happy about seeing her at such a difficult time.

As I was trying to avoid standing out in the funeral procession of people that came to express their condolences to my parents, I had taken refuge in a small room that was in the back of Robinson's Funeral home. That room was designated for the families to get away for a few moments or to meet with someone when they needed to have some privacy. I spent most of that day holed up there, trying to avoid any contact with as many people as I could.

I was sitting in that room, when my aunt walked in. She was the first to really ask me how I was dealing with all of it. She was kind and skilled at letting me talk as well as responding to me in terms that I could appreciate.

We talked for a long time. I finally confessed that I was concerned as to "where" my brother was at right now. I had gone to church a few times in my life. So, I had a basic idea of heaven and hell.

In simple words that I could understand, my aunt took the time to explain to me my need to have a personal relationship with Jesus Christ. I decided that day to accept the Lord into my life. It fundamentally changed my future and my life. I have no idea where I would have ended up if I had not found Christ in those formative years.

Again, this book is not about my faith. However, I would not be honest if I did not say something about it. It is the foundation that I have built my life upon and most of the decisions I have made in this life are based upon that personal relationship I have with Jesus Christ.

I am so aware of my failures in this life. Like most people, I have done things that I regret, and I should not have done. I so wish I would have been a better example of my faith to my friends and family. The truth is, many times I hid my faith and I never let people know how important it was to me.

The blog that I write is mostly about my faith. I will continue to write about my relationship with Jesus Christ and I plan to publish books about my faith in future endeavors.

12

ANGELS EVERY ONCE IN A WHILE

*W*inter was unforgiving in 1970. It had nothing to do with the weather, but rather the turmoil and trauma that our family was experiencing. No one in my family was looking forward to Christmas. We were less than a month from the tragic car-train accident that took the lives of our brother and cousin. How could we experience the joys that are associated with the season? It would be just another reminder that there were missing members of our family and emotionally none of us were in a place where we could handle that.

So, my family decided that we would take a trip to Florida to visit my grandparents. It was an escape from the obvious and while we knew that we still would never view Christmas the same way as we did previously, we knew that changing the scenery would at least provide enough distraction, so we could get through the Holiday season. We would take that trip and spend the holiday down in Florida.

I guess it served its purpose. We made it through Christmas and drove back to Ohio on New Year's Eve. I don't remember much about our time in Florida, other than giving my mom a present on Christmas day, and the memory of me, my mom and dad, along with my brother, Jim, and my sister, Linda, being crammed in a Volkswagen Beetle for endless hours as we drove there and back.

As a nine-year-old, I should have had the opportunity to experience a few more years of innocence and wonder when it came to the Christmas Season. But, I lost that magic that year and I never really got it back. I am not sure if it is the guilt that I feel, but there is a part of me that simply does not like to receive presents. It makes me feel uncomfortable and I always struggle with not feeling deserving of presents. It started that year and I never asked for anything specific for Christmas ever again.

It didn't start out that way. As a very young child, I would wait anxiously for Christmas morning to wake everyone up. I always thought it to be my responsibility since it was the assumed job for the baby of the family. As I look through boxes of old Christmas decorations, I am reminded of the Christmases of my childhood. I can remember each one since I was four. Every year, starting at Thanksgiving, I eagerly anticipated the coming Christmas season.

My earliest memory of Christmas was when my grandparents were making their annual trip down to Florida to spend the winter months. It was late October and they dropped off Christmas presents for all of us and we opened them early. After I opened my present, I was scurried off to bed and on my way, I said, "Merry Christmas, mommy." This has always been something my brother has teased me about my entire life. I guess October was too early to wish my mommy a Merry Christmas.

I was always so excited about Christmas and I learned that it was getting close when Santa, in all his glory, would be waving to everyone from the top of the Oak Harbor fire truck as it paraded through our little town.

As a child, I always thought it very suspicious that "Santa" would take time out of his busy schedule to ride around the little town of Oak Harbor. Considering that the only world I knew as a child was defined by the town limit signs, it made perfect sense that he would pick Oak Harbor to start the celebrations, even if I was a little suspicious about it.

I felt bad for the kids from other places because we had Santa here in our midst and they did not. All of us kids would be lined up — pressing our noses against the cold glass of the picture window, waving at Santa as he made his trek around town. Every child filled with visions of Christmas. Presents dancing in their heads and memories etched forever in remembrance.

It might just be my imagination, but it seems as if there were more homes with Christmas lights back in the day. As a kid, I would always look forward to the time when we would drive through town looking at all the lights strung across Water Street in the downtown area, as well as the many neighborhoods that were lit up. I still drive around Oak Harbor sometimes just to see the lights. It makes me feel rooted, a part of something in my past.

I remember that back then spending time "uptown" during the Christmas season was a celebration. Long before the "Mall" killed the small-town businesses, each local store would display sale items in their front windows. We would go window shopping to find items for our wish list. I can remember a year when I would stop and stare at this pair of ice skates in the Western Auto store window. I just knew that this pair of skates would make me the fastest skater at Gleckler's Pond. Oh, how I wanted them, but as Christmas came and went, the skates stayed in the window. We just couldn't afford them.

Each year, especially as we get older, things change and it's during the holiday season when you realize them. Most of the stores that once lined Water Street are no longer in existence. The 5 and 10 of W.R. Thomas, The Portage Store, Finke's, Van Atta's Restaurant, Lantz's Rexall Drug Store, Western Auto, Felhaber's Photography, Nehls Market, Faunce's Furniture, Hutchison Jewelry and the Modernette Gift Store to name a few.

To this very day, it brings a pain to a place in your heart where all your hidden feelings go. You mask it as "progress" but in your heart, you know that pieces of your childhood are fading into lost memories never to be remembered except for a picture or two. My children and grandchildren have been cheated. They will never get that experience of window shopping the same way I did as a child.

I remember running down the steps on Christmas morning and looking around the tree for the biggest box. I believed that within the biggest box under the tree would be the most expensive gift and best gift.

I always hoped it would be for me. But as time works its magic over the years in the mind and soul of a young man, I soon realized that every gift was special, unique, and meaningful. It isn't about the size of the gift, but rather the act of giving that brings the best feelings and memories of Christmas mornings. In fact, the presents that I remember most are the gifts that came directly from the heart. Christmas truly is not about the gift itself, but rather the thought behind the gift.

I learned this truth on a cold evening a few days before we left for Florida that Christmas in 1970. It had been a little more than a month since the accident and my mom was trying to go through the motions of the season for us kids but, as you can imagine, there wasn't a lot to be happy about.

I was nine. It was easier for me to be distracted by the celebration of the season than it was for my parents and my older brother and sister. But I knew. I knew that my mom was not the same. It was a struggle and she was drowning in the overwhelming loss of a child. I cannot think of anything more tragic. A parent is not supposed to outlive their child. It is something that I hope my family never has to experience again.

I could see that my mom was different. The sparkle in her eyes that I always remembered had dimmed. My nine-year-old mind tried to think of a way that I could make her smile again. I had never given my mother a present that I did not make on a piece of paper or a craft made at school. At that time, I really liked to color and draw and make abstract pictures. So, I sat down and did my very best to make the best picture I had ever done in my life. I was sure it would make all the difference in the world.

As a father, some of the most precious gifts I have ever received were the scribblings on a piece of paper made by my children. But when you're nine you start to think there is no value in that, so you want to do more. I looked at my picture that I put all my energy and creative energy in to and I just thought it would come up short in making my mom happy again.

I had saved $1.25 and I knew what I had to do. I had to go uptown and find her the perfect present. Something that would make her "smile" again.

Oh… the thoughts of a nine-year-old boy.

Somehow, I convinced someone to walk me uptown on that snowy afternoon. I was armed with cash and I was on a mission.

The Hardware Store was my first stop. As a child, when I would walk into the store, I would take a big whiff. I loved the smell of the hardware store. I was never quite sure what made those smells so intoxicating. Maybe it was the hot, oily machine parts from some of the equipment that they sold or just the decades-old hardwood floors of the store. I can only imagine how many spills of paint, turpentine, and oils that floor has absorbed. It's now toxic aroma is just hanging limply in the air along with metal nail dust, shiny tools, and plastic snow shovels. Yes, even as a child, as I walked those old hardware aisles, I soaked in memories. I remember clearly the creaking wooden floor and that jingle-jangly door clang as the door shut behind you. It was nostalgic then and even more so today.

I didn't find anything at the Hardware store for my mom that I could afford so we moved on to the 5 & 10 store. Now, one would think I could find something in that store for my mom. But, I just could not decide and was overwhelmed with all the options. I was confused and wasn't satisfied with any of my choices.

As a result, I suddenly found myself in Lantz's Rexall Drug Store. I was sure I was wasting my time there. The high school girl who worked there was trying so hard to find me something in my price range to get for my mother. It simply wasn't going to happen. I would have to go back to W. R. Thomas and sift through the options and find something back there.

It was at that moment, I now realize when you least expect it, angels appear every once in a while.

I hear a voice coming from the high window where a man was always standing whenever I was in the store. I never saw him ever come out from behind that Pharmacy window.

He asked me, "Are you one of the Lee boys?"

"Yes, sir," I said.

He came out from behind that window and walked towards me. He reached out to shake my hand and I noticed how warm and kind his handshake was.

He said, "How can I help you, young man?"

"Well, sir, I am looking for a present for my mom."

"How much do you have to spend?" he asked.

"All I have is $1.25," I replied.

"What are you looking for, son?"

I said, "I am not sure, but I want to get her something special."

He paused for a moment, looking around the store for options when he asked, "Does she like perfume?"

"Yes, sir, but I do not have enough money to buy something like that."

He reached up on the top shelf of the perfumes, grabbed a bottle, opened it and let me smell it. He said, "Do you like this one?" I nodded in approval.

He looked at me and said, "Well, son, this is your lucky day."

With a big, kind smile, he said, "This went on sale today and it costs exactly $1.25."

The high school girl who worked there wrapped my present and I gave the man my money and thanked him. As I walked out the door, I looked back, and I saw him still looking at me and smiling. I smile back, and he says, "Merry Christmas, son."

As a nine-year-old, I thought it blind luck to get such an expensive gift for my mom. It surpassed all my expectations. I have no idea how much that perfume cost, but I know it was more than the $1.25 that I paid for it.

Almost 50 years later, I realize that Mr. Mac McBain was an angel sent to help a little boy try and bring a smile back to his mother that had experienced tragedy.

It was all he could do.

I gave that present to my mom on Christmas Day. She smiled when she opened it. One of the first smiles I remember from her in a long time. She smiled to make me feel special. Now I know it didn't make everything ok and my mom wasn't instantly happy again. As a matter of fact, the smile and the sparkle in my mom's eyes were dim for many years. She did not really regain any joy in this life until her grandchildren were born.

I couldn't make things better for my mom, but as a young boy, it was all I had to offer.

Angels… every once in a while.

I believe that God allows it to happen just enough in our lives to allow us to keep faith in a loving God and the ability to hold on to the hope for a better world.

My angel that year was Mr. McBain.

He made the difference to a little boy who just wanted to make his mother smile again.

13

SCHOOL DAZE

Gilfillan, Provonsha, Milbrodt, Hetrick, Gula and Day.
Kind of sounds like a law firm.

No, this isn't a law firm, but I will tell you that a few of these people made me obey the letter of the law. These were my elementary teachers. Listed, in order, from kindergarten to fifth grade. I am not sure everyone can rattle off their elementary teachers in order like I can. I have asked friends and usually all I get in response is a blank stare as they stumble over trying to remember their teacher's names. Not me. While I still forget where I placed my keys a few times a week, I have always had the ability to remember my teachers in order and recite them off quickly. I always loved my elementary teachers. Each of them different, but each made an impact on my life.

When I decided to write these stories about growing up in Oak Harbor, I wanted to go and visit the places where these stories happened. I wanted to look to see if what I remembered was still there. Could I still see the places where I walked? Were the footprints of my past still there? The only answer was to go and see.

I got up on a Saturday morning and drove to Oak Harbor to visit R.C. Waters Elementary School. Since it was the weekend, I knew no one was around the school. I knew I could not walk the halls. I just wanted to take a stroll around the playground area and see what changed over the years.

I must admit I was nervous. Are you allowed to walk around the outside of the school that you started to attend over 50 years ago? I was convinced that the police would show up and ask me what I was doing, and I was preparing what I would say to them. I realized that it would be hard to explain why a 56-year-old man would be snooping around the elementary school.

I parked my car in the front lot. As I got out of my car, I was surprised that from the front view, the school looked exactly how I remember it from my first day of school in the fall of 1966. It is hard to explain the thoughts and memories that were spinning in my head. Suddenly, it was overwhelming, and a bunch of emotions were surfacing that I did not expect. I kept seeing places and faces that were no longer there.

As luck would have it, as I strolled around R.C. Waters Elementary school, I was not confronted by anyone or anything except memories of another time and place.

The summer of 1966, was a year of change for me. I was five and I was going to be starting kindergarten. The first few weeks in kindergarten are confusing, thrilling, and a little intimidating.

For the first time, you are on your own. You've been dropped off at school on your first day, and suddenly you find yourself in a new world. A world that is unfolding in a place other than your parent's house. You are at the bottom of the totem pole. You are among the youngest in the building. You're five, and in the hall way you see other students as old as twelve laughing and talking loudly and clearly familiar with each other in a way that you're familiar with no one... except for family.

You are thrust right in the middle of an unfamiliar place.

A place where you feel small, because you are.

The classroom, on the east side of the building, was always filled with noise and activity. For me, everything was new. The layout, the routine, the playtime, the random bells ringing in the hallways... nothing seemed remotely like anything I had experienced before.

My teacher was Mrs. Gilfillan. I wasn't too sure about her on my first day. Through my five-year-old eyes, she seemed old to me. I would run into her some twenty years later and she looked great and much younger than my eyes had placed her all those years ago. It's funny how perspectives change as you grow older.

We had been told each other's names, but all those names were hard to remember. Mrs. Gilfillan asked us to call out our own names every day as she took attendance. She was doing that on purpose... she already knew who was there and who wasn't. She was having us do the roll call out loud, so we would gradually become acquainted with each other. We were all challenged to put faces with the names. At that point in our life, we were not aware that most of us would spend the next 12 years getting to "know" each other.

I was shy, and it felt like everyone in the kindergarten room was more confident and sure of themselves. I sat next to a rather large boy... whom-- I'd soon learn-- was the class bully. Yes, even back then we had bullies. During those first few weeks at school, I got my initial lesson not only in just how cruel kids can be to each other but in how poorly prepared I was to defend myself.

After a few weeks, Mrs. Gilfillan scheduled a "Western Day" that allowed each student to dress up in a western outfit and bring something in for "Show and Tell." Now I admit the details of the event are a bit foggy, but what happened during the day is something that I have never forgotten.

I made my way into the classroom that morning and I started to hear some laughter coming from the play area of the kindergarten room. I looked up to see a group of kids staring at me and laughing. I made my way to my seat at the table I was assigned and didn't think much more about it.

I had worn a cowboy hat, boots, a plaid shirt and a holster that was made for two guns. One for each hip. However, I didn't have two guns. I only had one and it was broken, with tape holding the handle of the gun together. It never occurred to me that kids would make fun of another kid because he only had one gun... a broken one at that.

It was soon my turn to get up in front of the class to do my portion of the Show and Tell. I have no recollection of what my Show and Tell subject was because it was at this precise moment in time when I realized that getting up in front of a group of people would trigger my stuttering. It was also, the exact time I knew that I would do anything in the future to avoid getting up in front of people. I stumbled through my presentation and soon realized that I was getting laughter and giggles from some of my classmates directed my way.

It was time for the other students to have the opportunity to ask questions about my Show and Tell object. The first question was from the class bully.

His first question was, "Where's your other gun and why do you talk funny?"

I didn't know what to say. I was expecting a question about my Show and Tell and he was trying to make fun of me because I only had one toy gun in my holster and for the way I spoke. I attempted to respond, but I couldn't say the words and all I could do was start to cry. Mrs. Gilfillan quickly intervened and scolded the "bully" and calmed me down and allowed me to go back to my seat.

I don't remember much else of my time that year in kindergarten, aside from this strong memory. However, I can still feel it in my stomach to this day... the fear of speaking in front of people and the dread of mixing up my words. My issues with the way I "talk" in front of a group of people would haunt me throughout my school years and it would be a long time before I would speak up in front of the class again.

There is no doubt that I had some excellent teachers during my time in Oak Harbor. They would find a way to teach me and still deal with my issues. I am not sure that any of my teachers would remember me. If they did, it was for my issues and not for academic excellence. I was not what anyone would define as an academic scholar. I was an average student. I am so glad that my GPA did not define me. In life, they aren't going to ask you what your GPA was, and for that I am thankful.

I can only speak for myself, my teachers were a huge influence on what I would do in my life. Their influence goes much deeper than the lessons they ever taught me in the classroom. I never let any of them know what a huge impact they had in my life. They had no idea how much I looked up to them and hopefully, my grammar or my writing ability won't betray me, but I would indeed become a teacher and a school administrator. I loved every minute of that time in my life. I honestly felt like I was doing exactly what I was placed on this earth to do.

From personal experience, the most underrated and unappreciated job is being an educator. Without those who are made to teach, no one would be made to doctor, engineer or conduct business. Teachers lay the foundations upon which every child builds their goals. Without strong educators, a student's academic reach and potential is severely limited. Luckily for me, I was in the presence of amazing teachers.

My first-grade teacher was Mrs. Provonsha. She introduced me to some new friends called Dick, Jane, Sally and a dog named Spot. They would visit our class every day via a filmstrip presentation and in our reading books. I soon learned Dick and Jane liked to look a lot as well as run. Slowly, but surely, Dick, Jane, Sally and Spot were helping me to learn to read. I want to thank, Mrs. Provonsha for teaching me these foundational skills that I will use for the rest of my life.

Mrs. Milbrodt was my second-grade teacher. She is the one that taught me to write and put sentences together. I am forever grateful for her because she opened a door of adventure and perspective to a young boy that struggled with communication. She was also the one that explained the news to us and the political process of electing a president. That school year brought about Richard Nixon and an uneasy awareness of the Vietnam War.

Mrs. Hetrick, my third-grade teacher, taught me to love and commit to life-long learning. In the fourth grade, Mrs. Gula was my teacher. I am thankful for her for being patient with me and working so hard to get me back on track during a difficult time in my life.

During my elementary years, I am most thankful for Mrs. Day, my fifth-grade teacher, for making everything we did fun and for allowing me to feel normal again.

In junior high and high school, I must mention Vicki Sievert. She was my choir director. She was one of the few teachers that could relate to what we were all experiencing in our young lives. She worked hard at making me feel like I could sing, even though the evidence I showed by my attempts at singing proved that I could not. She took the limited talent that I had and encouraged me to work hard and try to do better. She was a wonderful example to me and I patterned how I handled students in my tenure as a teacher and principal after her.

My art teacher, Mrs. Cherry, was another huge influence on me. I can still see her roll her eyes as she would look at the lopsided ashtray that I would mold together, or the out-of-proportion drawing I would turn in each week for homework. She had patience and while I was never one that anyone would consider an artist, she continued to work with me. What I am most thankful for is the fact that she always had a knack for teaching me a lifelong lesson of how my art "failures" could relate to life. In addition, she taught me that I could find beauty in everything. Even if I needed to look deep into it to find it… it was in there somewhere. I have thought of her influence on me many times in my life.

But the biggest influence from a teacher came from my days in junior high. His name was Bernard (Bernie) Lutz. He was an English teacher.

He was hard. He was unfair. He was tough, too demanding and totally unreasonable. He was on a power trip. He was the equivalent of Oak Harbor's version of Attila the Hun. He was a "drop down and give me 20 pushups" kind of guy. He smiled on the first and last day of school and NEVER in between. Every student that had a class with him said the same exact things.

He was these things or worse.

But most of all… he scared me.

At least that was what I thought at the time. Unfortunately, the perspective of an eighth grader is somewhat tainted by the fact that at that age "everyone" who was an authority figure was considered the enemy. I mean it was the nature of a 13-year-old year to dislike that person who was trying to tell you what to do.

The truth is that Mr. Lutz was none of these things.

He was a teacher that "expected" things from his students. He wasn't going to accept average or below performance from you as a student unless it was indeed your best effort. More importantly, he was a great teacher who gave me something to think about at home besides homework.

Sure, he was hard, he was tough and he was demanding. He made mistakes and he was not perfect.

But never unfair, unreasonable or Attila the Hun.

It has been said that the mediocre teacher tells. The good teacher explains. The superior teacher demonstrates. The great teacher inspires.

For now, you see... Bernard... Bernie Lutz was one of the reasons I became a teacher. He was my inspiration.

My dream to become a teacher began with a man who believed in me, who tugged, pushed and lead me to the next plateau, sometimes poking me with a sharp stick called "truth." Looking back, I may have been naïve in my decision to teach, thinking what the general public may think also, 'how hard can it be?' To my surprise, it is the hardest, thankless job I ever ended up loving. I am grateful for the turn of events that led me to become a teacher.

Bernie passed away years ago. I never had the opportunity to tell him how much I appreciate what he did for me all those years ago. He never had a clue that I would become a teacher and consider him one that biggest influences on that decision. I am sure he never remembered me being in his class.

I've learned in teaching that you cannot see the fruit of a day's work immediately. It is invisible and remains so, maybe for twenty years or longer. The harvest for a teacher is seeing the "fruits" of their labor become teachers, lawyers, stock brokers, nurses, preachers, writers, accountants, bankers, managers, entrepreneurs and countless other occupations that make them contributing members of society. A teacher's influence never dies. Their legacy lives long past their time here on earth.

Bernie, thank you for influencing me. Thank you for helping me reach some of my dreams and helping me make a brighter future for some of my former students.

Maybe you were lucky, maybe there was a teacher in your past who believed in you. Someone who pushed you to another level. One who expected more from you than just average work or "just getting by." Someone who you never told how much you appreciate the challenge and inspiration they were in your life.

Let me go on the record of thanking the teachers that I had during my time in Oak Harbor. While I don't mention all their name's here, their influence is still evident in my life. There isn't a day that goes by that I don't think of some of you.

I encourage anyone who is reading this to take the time to thank their teachers. Tell them today. I missed my opportunity to tell my teachers thank you and how much I appreciate the sacrifice they made for me all those years ago.

14

THEY WALK AMONG US

The score was tied. The clock was winding down.

The game was on the line and the air was filled with electricity. Four... three... two... the basketball was in the hands of Ray Windisch.

He faced the defender and jumped, as he reached the peak of his jump, he raised the ball and with a flick of his wrist, he released a last-second desperation shot.

One... the ball left his hand just before the game-ending buzzer sounded and it rotated in slow-motion as it arched its path towards the hoop. The crowd, holding their collective breath, anticipating the results. At that exact second, there wasn't a noise that could be heard.

The ball cleared the front of the hoop and it made a "swishing" sound as the net snapped back as the ball rushed through it. The shot was good, and the noise that rose from the auditorium was deafening.

The Rockets were victorious once again.

In that precise moment, Ray Windisch became a hometown hero that younger kids would look up to for years.

Making a last-second shot to win the game for your hometown team was the dream of every single player that has ever played the game. In my mind, I can still see Ray make that shot. It was one the most incredible high school sports experiences I have ever been a part of. Ray will be etched forever in my mind as a "hometown hero."

It is what makes young boys and girls look up to upper-classmen and it motivates them to become just like the heroes they see on their high school teams.

I was no different, because watching that game on the stage-court of the old high school sealed my love for the game that I still carry. In the years following this event, I would make more heroes out of the players I would watch from the stands.

Besides Ray Windisch, there is another hero that comes to my mind to this very day.

It is funny how a kind gesture can stay with you. The smallest act a person does can resonate for years. That is what happened to me one cold day when walking from school to my Walnut Street home.

I was taking my time and not really paying any attention to anything. I was in my own little world, my head down as always and trying not to step on any cracks on the sidewalk.

I look up to see someone coming in my direction. Normally, if I saw someone coming up the same sidewalk, I would nonchalantly cross the street and try to make it look like it was a normal thing for me to do.

On this day, I had no time to make that happen. I was forced to cross this patch of sidewalk with whoever was walking up that sidewalk. I kept my head down and hoped I could walk by without being noticed.

There was no avoiding it, our paths were going to cross.

I looked up and it was Dick Wood.

He was a star player on the boys' varsity basketball team. Every Friday I would watch with envy as he would run up and down the stage basketball court that the Oak Harbor Rockets played on.

He was older than me, and in my mind, he lived in a different solar system than I did. The truth was he lived in my neighborhood.

As a star basketball player, he was everything I longed to be.

What was I supposed to do? Get off the sidewalk, to let him pass? Offer him words of praise? Ask for his autograph? I hadn't planned on this encounter. What were the rules for such an occasion?

What I did... was continue to look down at the sidewalk to avoid his gaze.

What he did... was say, "Hey David."

I looked up and he gave me a smile and a simple nod of his head as he passed by. No other words were spoken and in a flash, he was gone.

A small act on his part, but a huge event for a young boy who looked up to young men like him as role models and sports heroes. Young boys that thought if we were lucky enough we could someday be just like them.

So, here comes Dick Wood in his Christmas red varsity jacket with a big O-H in Christmas green and white on the front. He was larger than life and he was talking to me. He acknowledged me, knew who I was and actually said my name.

I couldn't help but smile. I could feel myself stand up a little straighter and my chest puff out with pride.

I started to run. I did not stop and when I got to my house, I burst through the front door, ignored my mom's request to close the door and proceeded to run through the house all the way upstairs to my bedroom.

I grabbed my rolled-up ball of socks that I used to play bedroom basketball and I starting shooting at the clothes hanger, shaped like a hoop, that was wedged in the back-side of my bedroom door. I had improved on the box I used to have taped to my door. I upgraded the box to a hanger. I was shooting and making shots from impossible positions. I played games in pretend scenarios that would always come down to Dick Wood making the last shot of the game as time ran out. In my bedroom, it was never me that made those baskets and be the hero. It was always Dick, and I would be there just to witness it.

It still gives me a warm feeling to know that, to this very day, Dick Wood had no idea what he did on that cold afternoon as he walked past me and said hello. He was genuine, and it was exactly what I needed. A simple "hello" from someone I looked up to.

I was a young boy that had withdrawn from everyone and everything.

He simply smiled, said hello and nodded his head.

Sometimes heroes and people we look up to aren't found outside the small town we grew up in.

Sometimes… they walk among us.

15

ANOTHER CHANCE TO GET IT RIGHT

*W*hen I was in fifth grade, there was a new boy named Darrell who came into our class. He was new to our school. He started about three weeks into the school year.

By that time in school, everyone had divided themselves into their own social subgroups and friends. Everyone already found a place to fit in. You usually hung with two or three other buddies and, for the most part, everyone got along. We had all grown up together and most of us had the same teachers since we were in kindergarten.

That in itself is a problem when living in a small town.

When we were young, knowing everyone in your class was something special. It was nice to always be familiar with your fellow classmates. But as you grow older, the inevitable sets in and you grow tired of the same people.

Maybe if he had his picture in our class composite he may have been remembered by more people. He didn't have his picture taken. He missed picture day and I probably would have forgotten all about him had I not had a life event that involved him.

I am ashamed to say that no one played with Darrell. He was an outcast. He was alone.

He was shunned by the whole class, and you would be shunned too if you sat with him at lunch or joined him in his solitary games at the fringe of the playground during recess. It was bad enough to have him in the same classroom.

All you needed to know about Darrell was that he was different. While his clothes appeared to be clean, it looked like he wore the same clothes almost every day of the week. He was loud, and it seemed to my 10-year-old thinking he was intentionally trying to keep people away from him.

He was ignored and over-looked, and he started to become the butt of cruel jokes and commentary that generally made up so much of the conversations of other fifth-grade boys.

I had never spoken to Darrell directly.

His family had moved into a run-down house just a few blocks from my own and I never once saw him riding his bike or even playing outside. As a matter of fact, I couldn't tell you if he even had a bike. Frankly, that's all I knew about him, and I thought that there was nothing else to know.

As the Christmas holiday approached, we drew names for our gift exchange. I was happy I did not get Darrell's name, and I began to wonder who drew my name.

I was so excited for our party on the last day of school before our Christmas break. I was also excited to finally know who had drawn my name and what I would be getting for my gift. Mrs. Day is my teacher and I am waiting for our Christmas party to begin. I waited anxiously and noticed that Darrell had given his tattered wrapped present to another student, so I knew he did not draw my name. I saw that he received his present from another student and I waited… but no one brought me a present.

My name had been drawn by another student that was absent that day. I didn't get a gift and everybody else noticed. Mrs. Day said, "Oh, that's okay. We'll make sure you get it when we get back from Christmas."

Bullies and time had already taught me all too well that you don't cry in public. Stuff like that wasn't supposed to matter. I strained to make myself look unfazed, but I remember how hot my face was and my throat was so tight that I could barely speak.

I felt like I had just gotten a big fat rejection notice.

All the other kids started playing some game. I stood off to the side trying not to throw up.

Out of the corner of my left eye, I saw some movement. I turned to see Darrell holding something out to me. It was a book-shaped box containing several rolls of Lifesaver candies. A common Christmas gift in that day. The sort of thing you grab at a checkout stand when you don't really want to think too much about the gift. Someone bought that present for Darrell.

He put it in my hand and said, "I want you to have this."

I just stood there. I didn't know what to say and couldn't have said it even if I had known. My throat was so tight I could barely breathe. Finally, I croaked, "But it's yours."

Darrell said, "And I've already gotten it. Now it's yours. Everybody should get something at Christmas."

I just stared at him, not because I was at a loss for words or was afraid I would cry, but because for the first time, I noticed how nice and kind Darrell was.

I tried to give it back to him. He refused, walked away and retreated to the same corner of the room where he would carry on conversations with himself and play his solitary games.

In shame that I carry to this very day, I was too afraid to say anything to anyone. I didn't even say thank you to him. I hid the gift in my desk and tried to assimilate back into my group of friends. All the while knowing that there was a boy playing by himself in the corner that was a much better person than I was.

Now, I wish I could tell you more about Darrell. I wish I could say that we had become fast friends and that maybe I had even helped all the other kids discover what a good person we had in our midst.

But that isn't the truth. I have not one single memory of Darrell after that. I learned that his family moved away over the Christmas break. Something, I am sure, he was used to.

Over time, the house that he lived in would remain empty and eventually be torn down.

I returned from that Christmas break, just as concerned about finding my own place in my little world of Oak Harbor, Ohio, and to avoid being the outcast and rejected.

In my own eyes, I was not enough. Sometimes, I was blinded by the effort to be accepted. Envy and intimidation blinded me at other times. There were times I was condescending, competitive or too preoccupied with my own fears and wounds and grievances.

Blindness to how you build your self-esteem becomes a habit.

We learn early in life to see only certain kinds of people. The ones who we think matter. We learn to look past or look through other kinds of people. Those who don't matter to us. I suspect we fear the stretching and growth that could be learned by the experience if we would see people as God sees them.

Darrell may have continued to be the ostracized loner, maybe he moved to Argentina or maybe he was abducted by aliens. Possibly he is the homeless man I pass along the way. He may even be my neighbor that currently lives a few doors down from me. He may be a doctor or a surgeon that has saved many lives. He may have been a solider that selflessly fought bravely for the freedoms I have enjoyed. He may have become a teacher that changed lives. Maybe he is the guy that works at the local factory. Maybe he is the mechanic that works on my car. He may have become a great husband and father that raised good kids. Kids that accept others who may be different from them. I have no idea. I'd like to think that many of these options are a possibility.

What I do know is this, a young boy that spent a few months in Oak Harbor, Ohio, in the early 1970's, was a better human being than I was.

I am concluding that even after all these years, I still have a lot to learn about acceptance. I have more to learn about loving people where they are in life.

I still have time to become a better person.

I still have another chance to get it right.

16

EVERY KID DESERVES TO BE A HERO

*L*ike many parents, I have spent many late nights at the park watching my kids play ball. Having my wife be at one game while I was at the other and then switching after three innings so that we could both see our children play are great memories.

My kids are now all grown and not playing ball anymore. I miss those times. They went by so quickly. For the past few years, I just drive to the park to get the feeling again. Every time I do, the memories flood my mind.

Often, I am taken back to my playing days… a long time ago…

As a kid, I loved baseball. I would play it as often as I could. Game days were the best. I usually spent most of the day dreaming of playing in the game that night.

Back in 1972, the ultimate sin on game day was the fact that we were forbidden to swim. (Is that still a rule?) So, since I could not swim, I would play out the game in my mind. With my whiffle ball and bat in hand, I took my place in my backyard playing out the many different situations of the game. In my mind, it was always me that was up to the plate at the crucial time… and like always it was me that delivered the mighty blow to win the game. I would be carried off the field in honor of my athletic feat.

Who of us hasn't dreamed of the getting the big hit, scoring the basket or catching the pass for a touchdown in the waning seconds of the game to secure the win for your team? I believe that it's every athlete's dream that has ever played the game.

On a hot July day, something happened that I have never been able to forget. It has been over 45 years since this event and it feels like it was yesterday.

Here is what happened.

That summer of 1972 I played on two baseball teams. I played for the VFW sponsored team in the Oak Harbor League, but I also played for the Merchants team that traveled to tournaments and played games all over North West Ohio. This was long before you had the "club" and travel teams that are in place today. The Merchants team was made up of the best players from the Oak Harbor League and we were good. While I was a good player, I was a bench player on the Merchant team.

The Merchants had a big game that day. We were playing the best team in the league. I did not start the game that day. I was charged to sit the bench until it was time for me to get in my required one inning of play. Don't get me wrong, in my backyard I was always the hero, but I was content to get my one inning and maybe one at-bat.

It was a very close game. We had the lead 4 to 3 in the top of the sixth inning. The coach had no other choice but to put me in the game. I was sent to my usual position and I just prayed to God that I would not have a ball hit in my direction. I did not want to be any part of losing the lead. I would just be happy to be able to celebrate with my teammates after the game. Three outs and we would win the game.

The events that caused our lead to dwindle had nothing to do with me. Not a single ball came in my direction. The other team scored two runs in the top of that inning. We were now losing 5 to 4.

As I ran to the bench after we got the third out, I looked up and saw my coach looking down at the scorebook. Then it hit me... I may have to go up and bat!!! I went over and looked at the scorebook and saw that I was scheduled to be the 5th batter.

"Ok, maybe we can score two runs before I have to get up to bat" I was hoping in my mind.

But fate would have its way that day. To my dismay, I was going to have to bat. We had one man on second base and one on third. Two outs and now it's all up to me. I reached down for the 28" bat I used and started my way into the batter's box. I am sure the sound of my knees knocking in fear could be heard in the stands.

I closed my eyes, reached deep down inside and gathered all the courage I had in my body.

"I can hit this guy," I thought to myself. All I needed to do was keep my eye on the ball.

After all, I had done this a thousand times in my backyard.

Just a hit…a hit would at least tie the game. If I hit it well, maybe I could score both and we would win the game.

"Don't over-swing…just make contact" I told myself.

As I dug my cleats into the dirt, I tried not to show my fear. I also did not want to look too confident. I only wanted to be the hero.

I settle into my standard Johnny Bench batting stance.

(NOTE: I am an Indians fan. Back in 1973, there wasn't a whole lot of players on the Indians squad that young boys would try to emulate. So, just like every other kid I knew, we took turns trying to look like Joe Morgan or Johnny Bench of the Cincinnati Reds)

First Pitch… here it comes… right down the middle… it's perfect… I grip the bat harder with my hands and start to swing and I suddenly stop myself.

"STRIKE ONE!!!" the umpire bellowed.

I didn't want to seem too eager…

"Make him pitch to you," I told myself as I stepped out of the batter's box. I reach down and grab a handful of dirt and rub it into the bat. I would be ready if he threw another pitch like that.

Next Pitch… here it comes… it's perfect!

SWING …

I'm not exactly sure how it happened, my memories begin with the crack of the bat, and the sight of the ball rising high into the crisp blue sky of summer.

My mind raced… "It was perfect, and I got all of it!" I thought to myself.

Then something happened that had never happened before. I don't know why I did it, but I did. I put my head down and start to head to first base. I was sure it was gone, and I started going into my backyard "home-run trot" around the bases.

As I round first base, I keep my head down and keep on my trot around the bases. Thoughts of being a hero were rushing through my head. I couldn't wait to hear the cheers from my teammates, coaches and fans. It was exactly how I played it out a few hours before in my backyard.

I reach second base and my teammate is still standing there. I wanted to tell him to run because I just hit a home run. But the look in his eyes told me something was not right. He was looking at me like I was the village idiot. Then suddenly I hear the sharp laughter of the fans, not to mention the cries of laughter from the opposing team.

"What happened? There is NO WAY they caught the ball," I thought to myself.

Then it hit me… no, they didn't catch the ball. It fell well short of the fence and in foul territory!

I stop my trot around the bases hoping to find a place to disappear. There is no escape from the snickers of laughter from the opposing team and those from my own teammates. I pan the crowd to see who exactly saw this and to my dismay… everyone.

I look to see my coach just shaking his head.

I really don't remember the last pitch, just the umpire yelling out, "STRIKE THREE!!!"

Over the years, I have told this story with many different endings. Sometimes, it's another player who does this embarrassing act. I then get to make fun of him. Sometimes it's me. I usually get a hit to tie the game. Not often, maybe once or twice, I told the story as if I hit the home run to win the game. I tell the story with as much conviction as any story I have ever told.

So, maybe it's not exactly what happened. But that's the way it should have ended, and that's the way I like to remember it.

We played more games that summer. I played in all of them. However, this is the game that comes to memory first when I think of those days.

And if dreams and memories sometimes get confused, oh well, that is as it should be because I believe that every kid deserves to be a hero every once in a while.

17

YOU ARE WHAT THEY SAY YOU ARE

*I*t was 1973 and I was a student at Rocky Ridge Jr. High. I was confident that this school year was going to be significant for me. This was the school year that I wanted to change. I wanted to impress. I was no longer an elementary student.

I had arrived... I was a seventh grader.

Bulletproof and 10 ft. tall.

Well... 4' 8" and 65 pounds, but still ready to take on the dangerous world that is known as junior high.

I spent the entire night before trying to pick out which clothes I was going to wear on that first day of school. Like many events in my life, I tried to imagine what it was going to be like. I was armed with my witty comebacks, cut downs and sarcastic comments that are typical of the junior high language. There was going to be a "new" me and I was sure I could pull it off. I wanted to be part of the "In Crowd," part of the "Cool Kids." All I had to do is get off to the right start and impress them.

There are a lot of things about junior high life that might seem simple to an outsider, but they're not. Take the 15 minutes before homeroom every morning. What you do with those fifteen minutes says pretty much everything there is to say about you as a human being. If you were cool, you had places to go and people to see; if you weren't, you'd start to wonder who you'd sit by at lunch.

When you were in elementary school, almost all of it was scripted. Your teacher told you where to line up and where to sit. You didn't get much say in where you would end up. I was wise to the fact that this would change in the seventh grade. We would be on our own when it came to where we would eat lunch and the teacher no longer made us line up in a certain order to get our food. I wanted to make sure that I found the right table to sit at. To make matter more complicated, all seventh graders in the school district would be going to the same school building for the first time.

The goal was to protect yourself, and safety came in numbers.

So, my plan was to find the "cool" table and, at all costs, avoid the table of "No Return."

The table of "No Return" is the table of kids that did not fit into any of the groups. You would have your group of "cool kids", a group of "smart kids", you have your "athletes (jock) group", and in those days, of course, you had your "band group", your "hoods" and your "nerds" groups.

Then you had a very small percentage of kids that did not fit anywhere in these groups. These were the people who sat at the table of no return. Meaning that if you sat there, you were destined to stay in this lost group with no identity. My fear was that is where you would find me... ostracized by all groups... even by the hoods and the nerds. I would just not belong.

Regardless of where you went to school, a junior high school cafeteria is like a microcosm of the world. The cafeteria was a representation of where you were on the totem pole of popularity.

These groups were even more splintered according to where you lived. We had a few small communities that all came together to go to the same junior high and high school. So, the communities of Rocky Ridge, Graytown, and Carroll Township would send their students to join with the Oak Harbor (town) kids in one building.

I would learn a set of unspoken rules when it came to where you sat during lunch. I was a "town" kid and there were rules that you had to follow. For example, there were no less than five different subgroups to each of these larger groups.

Let me explain… you had:

- Kids that lived in town (Oak Harbor)
- Kids that lived in Graytown
- Kids that lived in Rocky Ridge (Ridge Runners)
- Kids that lived past the Toussaint River (Toussangers)
- Kids that lived South of the Portage River

Kids from Graytown generally sat with the Toussangers and the Ridge Runners but did not sit with the in-town kids. Toussangers did not sit with the Ridge Runners but sat with the in-towners. Ridge Runners did not sit with the in-town kids. As for the kids from south of town and the Portage River…they sat in their own subgroup and sat by themselves.

I admit I may have this wrong and I tell this story through the eyes of a naive seventh-grader on the first day of school, but this is how I remember it.

While there may be a separation in the lunch room, make no mistake, only people from Oak Harbor can say bad things about fellow Oak Harborites. Like your family, you can say what you will about your brother but have someone else say something and there is a price to be paid.

So, according to my junior high school, who you are was defined, more or less, by who you were sitting next to during lunch.

In short, my initial 15 minutes in my homeroom that first morning did not go well and I found myself trying to find a place to sit in the cafeteria.

I make my way into the room. I can already see that the seating chart has already been established and it looks just like I thought it would. Groups were splitting off and tables were being claimed by each respective group.

I look left.

I look right.

Nowhere to go.

Nowhere to hide.

I make my way to the line and get my food. I smile and nod as I weave past the tables of no return, where some of my friends are calling my name. While I hear them, I act as if I can't and I head to the tables at the other end of the lunchroom.

I'm hoping that if anyone is watching me, it would appear that I am just heading in the right direction to meet some of my "other" friends at their table. I suddenly find myself at the other end of the cafeteria. There are no invitations. No call outs and it is obvious that I do not belong at the tables where I am standing.

The thought crosses my mind, "This is why kids drop out of school!!!"

I tell myself that the sole reason can be found at lunch. I am sure if anyone did an investigation as to why kids leave school it is because of the seating arrangements in the lunchroom.

I keep walking through the cafeteria because what else am I going to do? There are no empty tables, no empty seats and I've already passed all of my friends.

So, I backtracked my way back to my friends. They were kind enough to let me sit with them. If they knew I was looking to move and try to sit at another table, none of them said anything to me. They allowed me to come back and take my rightful, earned spot at the table of no return.

I sat with them every day of the school year.

In 7th grade, who you are... is what other 7th graders say you are.

As I reflect on my life in junior high in 1973, I am reminded that hometowns are like family - the shortcomings, flaws, arguments and disappointments are all there, but it is the love and loyalty of our true friends that make us who we are.

In this world of inconsistency and doubt, I have learned that home is what you make it. Most small towns in the late '60's and early 70's were all about the same. They were stuck somewhere between a fast-changing world outside its boundaries and the need to hold on to the values that made that small-town special.

Sure, some towns may have been a little bigger, and some may be a little greener, but there was only one real difference. Only one of them... was yours and Oak Harbor, Ohio was mine.

The funny thing is, forty-five years later, I still have fond memories of my seventh grade year.

And while I remember each name from my group of friends I sat with at the wonderful table of "No Return," I find it hard to remember the names of the other kids I spent so much time trying to impress.

18

OUR SMALL TOWN REMIANS RESILIENT

I've witnessed wonderful things that come from living in a small town. I am amazed at how much everyone feels the same way when we go through things together. When the high school team wins a tough game, we all are excited. We rally around the team. The cheerleaders decorate the halls of the school to promote school spirit and support for the team. It stirs up hometown pride and we feel like we are a part of the team too.

But the most remarkable thing I've ever witnessed is how we dealt with loss, grief, and pain. If you grew up in a small town, I am sure you'll be able to relate to the things I'm about to say.

The accident that took the lives of my brother, his best friend and my cousin was a defining moment in my life. Its impact was significant. It changed my family. It changed me forever.

My life moved in a different direction because of the tragedy.

However, it did not take long for me to realize that I was not alone in suffering from the grief and guilt of losing someone so young and so much a part of your life.

If you pause for just a moment and think about it, our little town has had so much more than its fair share of loss. Especially when it comes to losing young people. We have lost so many teenagers long before they ever had a chance to experience all the good that this life can bring. While these tragic losses have been surrounded by many wonderful things like sports wins, proms, and graduations, the times of loss always seemed to outweigh the good.

Anybody from a small town can attest to the fact that if someone in your town experiences a loss, it somehow becomes your loss. Why is that? In no way do we feel the hurt that the family and friends of this individual feel, but we see our community hurting and we empathize. It quickly takes us back to that time we experienced the loss of a loved one. Whether it was a sister, brother, cousin, friend, classmate, or significant other. We remember, and we hurt for the person going through the same thing.

This is a reminder that we are all connected in some way. You may not have known the person personally, but may remember them singing with the choir at church, or remember them coming to your house to play with your child. Your child may have ridden the bus with them, you may know their aunt from work, or their mom through a family friend. Either way, there's a connection, and when you think about all that person could have been or had been while here on earth, you're saddened.

When a loved one passes away in our small community, news travels fast. Tragic news from a single phone call spreads quickly. Hundreds of people across the area mourn because everyone knows everyone and is connected in some way.

Small towns have a reputation for everybody knowing your business, and for everyone being related in some way, but that's not always a bad thing. While people usually respond to this issue with an eye roll, this kind of connection results in a stronger community than I have been able to find anywhere else. At the end of the day, we stick together and support one another in times of crisis.

The list of children, teenagers and young adults from Oak Harbor that have died is devastating. I do not have a complete list, but I know that during my life, at least 40 young people have passed on from our small town. There may have been more. Many of them died after I left Oak Harbor, but that doesn't mean it still doesn't affect me. The list is so long that I could not mention them all. I fear that I would inadvertently leave one off the list. I never want to treat a life lived with so little concern that I might possibly offend one of the affected families.

So, I can only speak to those that had an impact on me during my time living in Oak Harbor. Again, please know this, I have no intention of offending any family or having anyone feeling slighted because I missed mentioning someone.

Regardless of how old or how they have passed on, each loss of a loved one is hard. However, the loss when they are young is the hardest. You don't expect people to be taken away from you so soon.

This chapter has been hard to write, but I remember being at the baseball diamond at R.C. Waters School waiting for the game to start when we were told to gather around the bench. Our coach told us that there would be no game that night due to a farming accident that took the life of our teammate, Jeff Hurrell.

I know exactly where I was when I was told that our classmate, Danny Neitz, had passed away. It was the first time I had ever known someone who died of cancer.

The September morning in 1974 after Scott Harder and Tom Apling were killed in a car accident was surreal because just a few days before I had talked to them about my brother Bobby's accident.

On December 4, 1971, five students were killed in a single car accident coming home from Penta County Vocational School. Those students, Jim Foreman, Tom Shanteau, Donald Whiting, Jim Pierson and Earle Douglas were all getting ready to graduate that spring.

Combined with my brother's accident, these represent 12 teenagers taken from a town of 2,500 in population in less than four years (1970 – 1974).

Again, there may have been more but these are the ones I remember.

There was another event that took place during those four short years of the early 70's that had a profound influence on me and on our little town.

I think it was about 9:00 AM when I heard the helicopter. It was loud and it sounded like it was landing right outside the window of our 8th grade Ohio History class. Mr. Morse stopped teaching and we all looked out the window of our classroom to see if we could see where it landed. We knew it was close because of the sound but we could not see it. Mr. Morse told us to stay in the classroom as he stepped outside to investigate.

After a few minutes, Mr. Morse returned and said that the helicopter landed on the practice field right next to the high school. He told us that a police car picked up a few people from the helicopter and they had left.

In a small town like ours, this was big news. I had never heard of a helicopter landing on the high school practice field before and we all were wondering what was going on.

As the day wore on there were rumors and stories floating around about who was in the helicopter. Some were saying it was someone famous and others were saying it was just someone visiting the mayor. What we would find out about why this helicopter landed in Oak Harbor would change how I slept at night.

In the early hours of November 12, 1974, a few area young men broke into a local bar in downtown Oak Harbor. They broke into a few coin machines at the bar and took a few bottles of alcohol. They left that bar and went driving around and after they finished off the bottles, they drove to the Northland Bait and Sporting Goods store located on North Locust Street.

Around 4:00 AM, they removed a side window and entered the store. They were going to steal some guns and ammunition and during that process a hunting decoy was knocked over. This woke up the owner's dog and it started to bark.

After the dog started to bark, Mrs. Musser, the owner, came down the stairs to see why. Unknowingly, she walked into an ongoing burglary. The young men that were involved immediately pulled out the handguns and rifle they had just stolen and pointed them at her. She was then led to the back of the store where they took a scarf and made it into a blindfold and covered her eyes. They had been in the store before and they were afraid that she could identify them.

Gretchen Musser, along with her husband, was the owner of the bait store. I knew Mrs. Musser and she knew me. Also, she knew my brother Bobby before he died.

I used to go to the store often. Sometimes to buy a pop or some candy after playing football or baseball games with the kids that lived at the north end of town. Also, I would go to the store when Kenny Wheeler, our next-door neighbor, would take me fishing with him. We would stop in the store and buy worms and tackle for our fishing trips. She wasn't always working in the store, but she was there enough for her to know that I was the youngest Lee boy.

These men kidnapped her and took her with them when they left the store.

The helicopter that landed just outside of the school that morning was the FBI that came to assist the local police in finding Mrs. Musser. All the authorities knew was that there had been a robbery and that she was missing. For our little town, this was devastating. We never even considered locking the doors to our house, let alone comprehending the horror of someone kidnapping another person.

News travels fast in a small town. It wasn't long before the whole town was aware of the situation and the shock wave of fear had made its way to each home. Suddenly, people were locking their doors and keeping their lights on all night.

Everyone was on alert. Questions that this small town never had to face before were on the mind of every person. Who could have done this? Why did they do it and most importantly, where was Mrs. Musser?

Those questions would be answered three days later when one of the young men who was involved confessed to the police what happened.

Within a half-hour after breaking into the store, they took Mrs. Musser to a barn a few miles away and took her life.

For the first time, I realized the evil that people can do. Up to this point in my life, I had never known evil in our small town. Sure, I had endured and experienced tragedy and loss, but not pure evil. Those things happened in big towns, cities and other places. It was something that you heard on the news, or read in the newspaper. It wasn't found a few blocks from your home.

I think of Mrs. Musser often. I have not forgotten a wonderful woman that just wanted to live long enough to see her grandchildren. She was cheated out of that. She was cheated out of a full life by the hands of a few young men.

For a long time, there is no doubt that the events that took the life of Mrs. Musser, changed our town. Suddenly, people withdrew and kept to themselves. I stopped knowing all the names of people that moved into my neighborhood. Porch lights that once offered warm invitations for everyone to visit, were now burning cold and protective. They were now used as shields of defense to keep people away.

It took a while for it to get back to normal, or should I say, the "new normal." I am not sure we ever "got back" to how it was before that November day in 1974.

Once innocence is shattered, it cannot be put back as it once was.

Most people never stopped locking their doors and porch lights still functioned as security lights. As a community, we have withdrawn and do not know the person that lives down the street.

Personally, I have locked my doors every day since that day.

However, this truth remains… in difficult times, our small town remains resilient.

We rally around each other in times of tragedy and the loss of loved ones, regardless of age.

My hope and prayer is that even with our differences and perspectives, the values and way of life that was established when the village of Hartford was founded will forever be found in the people of Oak Harbor.

19

A MOMMA'S BOY

There were no two ways about it. When I was fourteen… I was a cool kid, or at least I thought so.

I knew the walk. I knew the talk. I had my own kind of… style.

But, like a lot of kids at fourteen, I did have one tragic flaw. One terrible secret that threatened the very fabric of my fragile image.

One secret that most teenagers try to hide…

I, David Michael Lee, was a momma's boy.

When you're a little boy, you don't have to go very far to find the center of your universe.

That was your Mom.

She's always there, no matter what happened in your life, and it's a pretty good arrangement. She was there when you went to bed, when you got up in the morning, when you left for school and when you came home. As a young boy, all you can imagine is the fact that you will be with her for the rest of your life. Nothing would ever change that. She would always be there and never leave your side. I would always be momma's boy and nothing could change that.

But around age fourteen, there starts to be… a problem.

The problem then is…she's always there. And I mean always.

She poured my milk, she sewed my buttons… face it, the woman loved me. She knew me better than anyone in the world. Which, of course, was the problem. She knew… too much.

Now a mom must be a mom, but a guy must be a guy. And when the irresistible force of independence meets an immovable object… sooner or later – something has to give.

Unfortunately, it did.

I guess I could tell a story of how we ended up having some big terrible fight or some extreme family crisis and that we didn't talk to each other for years and we would reconcile years later… however, none of that would be true. It may be a better story to be read than the one I'm telling…but what took place is something a little more sinister. Something more hurtful. Something filled with more regret.

I did what teenagers have done since the beginning of time.

I did something that I can never take back.

I ignored her.

When I say, I ignored her; I mean I took her for granted. I did not take the opportunity to spend more time with her. I started to make my own decisions and I left her out of most of my plans.

I did not do it intentionally.

It wasn't meant to hurt her.

It was a part of growing up and I regret it to this very day.

20

PAINFULLY PERFECT

For my friends and me, our freshman year looked like it was going be a smooth year for us. We weren't 8th graders anymore. We no longer considered ourselves "boys" but men. More importantly, we were men among freshmen girls.

Sometimes in high school in our little town, there were days when you felt like there was nothing much worth getting out of bed for. But then, you remembered you were going to see… her.

Your day was going to have all these moments that were full of possibility. You just knew that you would see her in the hall. You hoped to catch a glimpse of her as she walked into the cafeteria. Maybe, as the both of you switched classes between science and math class, there would be a possibility of catching her eye and giving her a little smile. Not too big… just enough to send the message of approval. All you could do was hope that she didn't catch you staring.

Ahhh… fourteen… you're too young to vote but old enough to think you're in love. You live in a house someone else owns. Your dreams are somewhere else, and you are already planning your escape from the tiny confines of that small Ohio town. You face the future armed with nothing, but the money earned from mowing lawns, a three-dollar corsage, and a light blue leisure suit.

And you hope against all hope that it will be enough.

There are very few things in life as purely terrifying as calling a fourteen-year-old girl on the telephone, especially a cute fourteen-year-old girl. I asked, and she said yes.

Her parents would only allow her to go if they could drop her off and then pick her up after the dance. I agreed and as much as that kind of stymied my expectations and ruined most of my plans for the perfect date, I was still excited. I would meet her at the school for the dance on Saturday night.

Now, most people don't know this but there are two kinds of logic. There's logic-logic and then there's fourteen-year-old boy logic. I was sure that nothing bad could happen. At least nothing that would leave a permanent mark. Had I known then what I know now, I would have walked the other way.

So, that Saturday, I stood there in my light blue leisure suit with my new floral silk shirt. We met in the middle of the hallway. The same hallway that we passed each other every day for months. She walked into the hall with a beautiful red dress on. She looked just as I pictured in my mind, she looked beautiful.

I gave her the three dollar-corsage and we entered the dance. The measurement of success that night was more about the entrance to the dance than the actual dancing. All eyes were fixed on the door for the next couple to come through the paper mache streamers. We made the grand entrance and for a moment the world was spinning and revolving around us as we made our way into the room. We were the center of the universe.

It was painfully perfect.

It was wonderfully uncomfortable.

It was terribly frightening.

Not a word was spoken. Suddenly the things we talked and joked about at school every day were now void. The more we tried to talk, the longer periods of silence would follow. We were too young and neither one of us knew how to handle the pressure. We forgot that we were there to have fun. It was forced, and I had no clue as to how to fix it.

After the third song, we finally made it out to the dance floor. We slow danced to a song I cannot remember. And then she was gone. She had taken refuge in the safe confines of her freshmen girlfriends and I found myself standing with the other lonely freshman boys.

And so that happened.

I knew that there would be other dances but in that moment my immature, fourteen-year-old heart crumbled into a little pile of dust and blew away.

The dance for me was over.

I still had a little self-respect. I was not going to stand there with all my other friends and watch our dates giggle, laugh and dance together in their little group at the other end of the dance floor. I walked down to where my date was standing and I was going to tell her it was ok, we didn't have to dance. She said that she wanted to be with her friends for a while. I told her that I understood but I knew that it was time for me to leave.

I managed to slip out the side door without being noticed. I walked towards home. I put my head down as my mind raced to make up a story as to why I would be home so early. I knew I had a few blocks before I would have to face the music with my family.

As I walked past St. Boniface School on my way home, I suddenly heard voices. I heard laughter. I looked up into the darkness and saw a few of my friends. A few had left the dance and met up with some of our friends that did not go. They were just hanging out. A few were even swinging on the swings. Some were climbing and playing on the monkey bars on the playground. Something none of us had done since our elementary days.

Maybe we all realized that growing up doesn't have to be so much a straight line but maybe a series of advances and retreats. Maybe we were learning that we were growing up too fast. Maybe it was the fact that we missed something about our childhood. I don't know, maybe we just felt like swinging. But whatever it was, my friends and I made an unspoken pact that night to stay young for a little while longer even if it was only for a few more hours. There was no need to rush.

The responsibilities of growing up and the desire to find love would come soon enough. I was just starting out on my journey to find it. I wasn't even sure I knew what it was anymore. But I knew I had a lot to learn and my quest to finally find it was a long way off. Love and all its responsibilities would have to wait.

Years passed and my quest to find love would be fulfilled along the way as I journeyed through life. It was everything I had hoped it would be and more.

The funny thing is... forty years after this experience, I still find love to be... Painfully Perfect, Wonderfully Uncomfortable and Terribly Frightening.

21

IT'S A LONG WAY TO CLEVELAND

*E*veryone needs a place to go to be a kid. For my buddies and me, that place was ten minutes from home if you walked it. It was a world all its own. All the kids from our neighborhood would gather there. It is where the boys learned about girls and it's where the girls learned how immature the boys were.

All of us grew up there.

Together.

That summer, the place to be was Teagarden's Pool.

So many things happened there... so many memories. But of course, none of it was permanent, unless you count the flashes of images and thoughts of a time not cluttered with the responsibilities of adulthood. Each day was filled with shrieks of laughter and catcalls as me and all my friends would swim on endless summer days. Sure, they called it Teagarden's Pool, but we knew better. That pool... belonged to us.

On one beautiful day in June, I was at the pool to take a Junior Lifesaving course. I had known how to swim since I was five. I had worked my way through the Tadpole, Guppy, Dolphin, and Shark divisions. Now, I was on my way to becoming a "lifeguard." Looking back on it now, I probably took all those classes because they were taught by girls, not just any girls... but older girls... girls in bikinis.

On this summer day, this pretty girl was there to take the class. Now, I knew all the girls in my age group from our little town of Oak Harbor, Ohio. But this girl wasn't a girl that I knew. She was "new". A rare find in our little town.

I tried not to look like I was staring. I quickly looked away if I saw the slightest twitch that she may look in my direction. I sat there trying to look like I was paying attention to our "instructor-in-the-bikini", but I couldn't stop looking at the beautiful stranger that was dropped from heaven. Who was this new girl? Where was she from? Where was she living and, more importantly, was she staying?

Apparently, I wasn't the only one whose eyes were fixated on the new visitor. I looked at the class and every hometown girl who was taking the class was staring as well. The evaluation was in full motion. As my eyes, and all the other boys, were looking in approval, the other girls there were judgmental and critical of the new-found competition.

As fate would have it, when it was time to break up into groups for our first activity of the class, I was placed in the same group with her. I couldn't believe it, what luck! She was walking in my direction and my mind was racing a million miles per hour. I was going to be the first to talk to her. I was desperately trying to think of something witty to say, something profound. Something to break the ice… something to let her see I was a "cool" guy.

I was sure I did not want to say something like "Hi, my name is David. What's yours? Where are you from? How old are you? Why are you here? Did you move here? Why are you taking this class?"

No… I did not want to say these things… but I did. As a matter of fact, I said it without taking a breath and yes, I said the whole statement in less than 1.2 seconds. A world record I'm sure.

She was just staring at me. The look on her face was evident that she believed she just met Oak Harbor's village idiot. Her jaw dropped, and I could see that she was trying not to laugh at the jumbled mess that just came out of my mouth. She was trying to respond, but could not for fear that she would make fun of the village idiot. So, she spoke in precise, deliberate and painfully slow words. She spoke loud. You know, like when you talk to someone who is deaf or from a foreign country. Like somehow if she talked louder, I would be able to understand what she was saying.

"MY NAME IS KAREN!!" she slowly exclaimed.

It was evident that I lost any chance of convincing her that I was a normal "cool" guy. So, I relaxed. I interrupted her and told her that I wasn't deaf, and I was at least smart enough to follow what she was saying. I tried to be coy and told her I might not understand everything she said but I would at least try. She told me she was 15 and was from Cleveland. She was camping at a local campground for few weeks with her grandparents. She was bored at the campground, so they let her take this class.

I was so glad that she didn't catch me staring at her. I mean, I already made an absolute fool out of myself; I did not want her to think I was a pervert as well.

Maybe she was just a kind-hearted soul that took pity on village idiots or she indeed liked being with me because for the next two weeks we were inseparable. I would wake each morning and hurry down to the pool at 8:00 AM and sure enough she would be waiting there for me.

After class, we would stay at the pool until it closed at night. We would swim and talk for hours. We never left the pool. Karen told me about everything in her life. She told me about her school, her friends, and her family. She never had, or wanted, a boyfriend. She told me how her father died when she was two and her mom had recently remarried a man she did not like. He made her feel uncomfortable. He was always making comments and touching her in ways that made her feel uneasy. That was why she was in Oak Harbor in the first place. She was trying to get away from some things she did not want to deal with.

We talked and talked. I didn't mind. She told me things that she said she never told anyone else. I guess in some way, I made her feel comfortable. Maybe she knew that she could say exactly what was on her mind and not feel judged because of it. She was sharing her memories, feelings and dreams as she spoke to me.

At times, she would stop talking and get real quiet. She wanted me to talk to her about my life. We would talk about my brother's death and life in a small town. We talked about religion and what we believed. We shared our love for music and what we wanted to do for the rest of our lives. It was special because we could talk, knowing that we could say anything, and we would not be judged like we would have been had we been talking to our friends that we grew up with.

And we both knew… it wouldn't last forever.

Soon that inevitable time came upon us and neither one of us wanted to admit what was taking place. She had two more days before she was going to go back home. It was Friday and she would have to leave Sunday morning. As the pool closed that warm summer Friday night, we stayed a little longer talking at the gate before her grandparents picked her up. She looked nervous and I asked her what was wrong. She just looked at me and stared. With the sun setting in the distance and the color of her blue eyes reflecting off the last remaining rays of light, she looked up and kissed me.

No, it wasn't my first kiss. Maybe it was her first kiss, I don't know. But I do know that this was different. This was not about a boy and a girl. In fact, in the two weeks we spent together we had not as much as held hands. This was about friendship and the special time we spent together.

She placed a letter in my hand and asked me to promise not to open it until I got home that night. We had one more day together and we made plans to meet the next day at the pool, like always.

And in an instant, she was gone.

I took my time walking home that summer night. I wanted to remember and etch it in my memory. I read her letter. She wrote of our first meeting at the pool. She told me that she thought it was cute how I kept staring at her that first day and how I tried to look away when she looked over at me. She had caught me staring!! I thought I had hidden it. She wrote about the pool and all our talks we had. She told me she would miss me. She told me goodbye. Her grandparents were leaving early on Saturday morning, not Sunday. She wouldn't be coming back to the pool.

I knew at that moment, that life was not fair. In the haste of the last night together, I never got her address. It was hopeless. I think she wanted it to end this way. When you're fifteen, Cleveland is so far away. It might as well have been on the other side of the world.

I'd never felt like that before in my entire life. The next day I ran down to the pool in the fleeting hope that she would be there. Maybe there was a chance she would stop by before she left for home. She wouldn't come to the pool that day. Our time together that summer was over.

That was over 40 years ago and even today, I think about a friendship that lasted for two weeks that I have carried with me for all these years. I wonder whatever happened to her. I wonder what she would be doing now and if some of her dreams had come true. I wonder if she still thinks about a skinny kid from Oak Harbor, Ohio.

I like to think so.

I kept that letter she wrote me in an old shoe box. Over the years, I took it out every now and then, unfolded the tattered, yellowed pages and was immediately taken back to another place and time. Suddenly, for a few moments, I was fifteen again and life wasn't filled with the responsibilities I have today.

I have no idea where that letter is today. It was probably thrown out with the trash when I wasn't paying attention to what was in that old shoe box.

But I still have the memory.

Memory has a way of holding onto the things you love, the things you are and the things you never want to lose.

It also holds the frustration you feel when you realize that it's a long way to Cleveland when you're fifteen.

22

FRIDAY NIGHT LIGHTS

A few years ago, I returned to see an Oak Harbor football game. I hadn't been to a game in over 25 years.

There was a time when Friday night football was the center of existence. Most of the downtown merchants allowed the cheerleaders to paint their storefront windows with images that would encourage and promote school spirit. The cheerleaders would then decorate the player's lockers, paying close attention to detail and doing a little more for the senior football players. The school colors of Christmas red, green and white would flood the hallways of the school. Pep rallies were held to encourage everyone to get involved in support the football team. On game days, the players would spend the whole day wearing their jersey around school, counting down the periods until school was finally over so they could focus strictly on the game.

The players knew that growing up in Oak Harbor meant they were born and raised for those Friday night lights. It seemed like every kid would dream of the day when they would play under those lights.

No one took anything for granted because they knew the history of what the teams and players had done for Oak Harbor in the past. Nobody wanted to let the town down! Every player that ever put on that Rocket green helmet knew who they were playing for: their teammates, their families, the school, the town, and for all former Rockets that ever wore the uniform.

A lot can change over the years.

I pull into the parking lot and slowly get out of my car. There is something that is always uncomfortable about walking into a football game by yourself. It's like there is an unwritten expectation that you go to the game with someone else.

I am alone, and I feel self-conscious.

It's October. There should be a chill in the air but there isn't. I expected the school colors to be draped all through the stadium and everyone standing shoulder-to-shoulder like I remembered the games in my memory. But tonight, the attendance is sparse, and the stands are mostly filled with just family and friends.

I wonder where the students are? Back in the day, I would not miss a game. There was something about walking around the old stadium on the corner of Walnut and Church Street. The bright lights glowing in the dark night, illuminating the field where football dreams and legends were made. The area behind the stands were so dark that, at times, you had a hard time seeing who people were until you were right up next to them.

I would wear my two-sizes too big, red varsity jacket. I was so proud to wear that jacket. Jim Blausey and I were the first in our class to receive our varsity "letter" and as soon as I bought my jacket from the Portage Store uptown, my mom sewed the OH letters and class numerals on to my jacket. For a few years, I am not sure I wore another coat. I still have it hanging in a closet. Every now and then, I get it out and hold it in my hands and remember the pride I had when I got that jacket.

I usually stood next to bleachers where the band was. I always thought that was the best place to see and be seen at the game. Right in front of the cheerleaders where I could have a chance to check out the girls in the band. I always had a thing for girls that played in the band.

When I was much younger, I was usually playing football with my buddies on the practice field just east of the scoreboard. As we would play, we were sure that it was preparing us to one day play for real for the Rockets. We were also convinced that during the real game, the coaches were keeping an eye on the valiant football feats that were taking place just yards from the main field. It was our dream for all of us to play for the Rockets and be part of the tradition.

Tonight, however, I felt like a visitor and I was trying to find a seat where I would not be recognized. I suddenly hear the band playing. The band is playing the Oak Harbor "fight song" and unexpectedly I am adrift in nostalgic familiar territory. I stop and listen, and I am surprised that words come oddly back to mind easily...

"We're loyal to you OH High..."

I then watch the band march off the field to the same drum cadence that has been the signature of the band for as long as I can remember.

"O-H-H-S... O-H-H-S... Rockets!!!"

I make my way to the front of the stands. My brother and sister are somewhere in the crowd. They are here for their class reunions. For my brother, his 45th. My sister, she is back in town for her 40th reunion. My brother has only missed probably 7 or 8 games of Rocket football since the day he graduated all those years ago. He is a walking history book of Oak Harbor football knowledge. He knows and remembers all the players, the teams, and their stat history. For my sister, this may be the first football game she has been to since she walked off the field on her last game as a cheerleader her senior year.

I find them with their respective classes in their designated seating so that they can sit together and talk about old times and watch the game together. I am keenly aware that I don't belong to either of these classes. But I wedge myself into a seat among them and suddenly I am an imposter. It feels like everyone's staring at me. Each alumnus from the class of 1971 and 1976 trying to figure out who I am.

A face they don't remember.

My sister reminds a few people who I am sitting with, that the person who has crashed their party was her "little brother" and for some, a vague sense of recollection comes to mind. I am sure they found some relief in knowing that I wasn't someone in their class that they totally did not remember.

The game has already started, but I can't follow what's happening on the field. The sun has long set, but the lights are so powerful that it looks like the type of daylight I often experience in dreams.

Surreal. Metallic. Unforgiving.

Friday night lights.

I am sitting amid a group of people who are themselves trying to reconcile their memories of the past to the reality that is surrounding them.

I am no different.

My mind starts to drift off... suddenly it is 1973.

It was the first day of football practice – I was late.

I began to panic.

Maybe I'd come on the wrong day! Maybe I'd come to the wrong place! Every time I would open a door, there was another hallway. I couldn't find the coaches – I couldn't find any of the other players. That's when it hit me, this was junior high school and the transition from elementary school to junior high was a BIG deal to me.

And I was completely alone and on my own.

It was 1973.

It was a crazy time. Nixon and the Watergate scandal were the headlines and people were on the move... asking new questions... looking for answers. People were breaking new ground and wanting a change and it seemed like everyone I knew was searching for a new identity. Including me. That September, I entered Rocky Ridge Junior High. I was looking forward to new adventures. I wanted to start my football career with a bang.

My summer baseball season had ended on a sour note. I was clearly given a sign from the baseball gods that my dreams of being a baseball player were dashed upon the rocks of reality and I was looking for new opportunities. I wanted to play sports, but not just any sport, the sport of football to be exact.

I had always idolized the high school football team. I would always think about what it would be like to play in front of my friends and family. Playing on Friday nights, in the glow of the bright lights that would spotlight hometown heroes and legends.

I spent many Friday nights watching the game from the railroad tracks that ran along the west side of the field.

I would wait patiently until halftime and then they would close the ticket booth and we were free to enter the game. For me, Oak Harbor's football stadium at the corner of Church and Walnut will always be considered hallowed ground and it was the players and teams that made it special.

In 1973, the junior high football team changed into their practice uniforms at the high school on Church Street and after running down every hall of the school, I finally found the locker room and went in.

To say that they were less than pleased to see me come into the locker room more than 10 minutes late for the first day of practice is an understatement. For what it's worth, it did get me noticed. Linda Lee's little brother. More importantly, I gave the coaches a face of the one person they would ride and harass for the rest of the season.

I survived that first day and at the end the week, the coaches called out my name and threw me my football jersey. Christmas green... with the number 80 blazoned in white on the front and back. I was now officially a member of the 7th-grade football team for the Oak Harbor Rockets.

I was so proud.

I had not even put on a pair of shoulder pads yet, and here I was strutting around in my football jersey. I was way too cool, and I remember walking about two feet off the ground. I had no clue of what I was going to face in the coming days.

Considering the fact that in 1973, I was a smidgen over 4' 8" and weighed all of 65 pounds, I should have been keenly aware of what I was about to face. We were lined up in the hall outside of the equipment room and waited for our turn to be called in to be fitted. I was so excited.

Names were called, and I waited patiently. I was among the last 5 or 6 players that were called. When I was finally fitted with my equipment, I realized that something was different. Before I ever stepped onto a field with football pads on, my fate had already been determined. While the bigger kids and those who had families that had special ties to the school received newer equipment, I was given football pads that were straight out of the 1950's. My way too large helmet was commonly called a "monkey ear helmet" because of the protruding ear portion of the helmet.

"That will work!!!" my coach declared, as he slapped the side of my monkey helmet. The helmet spun so far that I was now looking out the earhole of the helmet. But all my thoughts and concerns were about one day playing under the lights on a Friday night. So, I straightened out my helmet and made my way to the door of the locker room.

I almost made it out when I was stopped because a father was in a heated argument with the coach about the inept, outdated and unsafe equipment his son had been issued. A few minutes later that son would emerge with nice, appropriate equipment and a rounded safe helmet like the Varsity players wore.

I didn't have parents that did that kind of thing. I was completely alone and on my own.

Still, I was proud. I was starting my time playing football. I wasn't going to let inept, outdated and unsafe equipment get in my way. I did learn quickly that running around with all these pads on was much different from what I was used to when the guys and I played backyard football in Blakely's yard. This was going to take some time to adjust.

For the most part, I survived the first few practices by being lucky and except for the prodding from the coaches, I stayed out of the line of fire. Then the fateful event happened. We had a football drill called "hamburger" which basically is a drill where two players lie on their backs with their helmets touching. On the coach's whistle, both players get up and run back four yards in opposite directions, where one player takes a handoff from one coach and the other slaps the hands of a waiting coach. At that point, they turn and run at each other. The player with the ball tries to run through the tackler and the tackler tries to bring the ball carrier down. After the tackle is made, each player moves to the back of the line because all players take part in this drill.

I took my spot in line and as I got closer to my turn to participate in the drill, I looked across to the other line to see who my competition was going to be. I really wanted to make a good impression on the coaches and I wanted to make sure I was matched up with someone my size and if luck would have it, maybe even someone smaller than me. So, I watched to see who was going to line up against me. I saw that it was someone who was bigger than me and I started to shuffle my way to a spot further back in line where I would be matched with someone closer to my size.

I got to my preferred place in line when I heard the loudest whistle I think I have ever heard. Then I hear my coach screaming out my name, "LEE... front and center!!!"

I had been caught cutting the line... which was a big no-no.

He grabbed me by the facemask of my "monkey ear helmet" and proceeded to pull and drag me back and forth in front of my team. All the while using me as an example as to what a player was not supposed to do at practice.

After the verbal tirade and personal humiliation, he finally pulled me over to the spot where I would have to carry the ball. He made me lie down on the spot and I know he is talking to the other players, but I cannot hear what he is saying. The whistle blows, and I jump up to take the handoff from my coach. Everything is good up to this point and I take the handoff and turn to run the ball through the defensive player. Here is when things start to go south, because it is then, I see him.

Earl Kashmere... that's right, and he was a monster. Earl Kashmere was Mr. Football of the Oak Harbor Junior High. He was no less than a foot taller than me and he was about 100 lbs. heavier as well. Earl was just staring at me, waiting for the kill and I thought just before he hit me that I saw a glimpse of a small smile come across his face.

I had never been hit so hard in my entire life. My entire body went completely numb and I saw stars, once again, through the earhole of my helmet. I remember hitting the ground and as all the air rushed from my lungs so did any current desire to play football.

I never told my family what happened. I am sure it would be a lawsuit by today's standard. Back then, coaches got away with that sort of thing. I didn't have anyone to tell and I surely did not have helicopter parents that protected me. I would have just been told that it would build my character.

Have you ever known those moments that changed your life? Do you remember a specific time, a special event that was life-changing for you? I think it happens to all of us, I know it happened to me on that day. I suddenly realized that football wasn't for me.

I would never play under those hallowed lights on Friday nights.

I didn't quit. I stuck it out for the season. I wanted to play, but I just wasn't good enough or big enough. So, I finished the season and the dreams I had of Friday night lights faded off into the distance.

Profound moments of life are not all good moments.

So, my football career was short-lived, and I never played football again for the Rockets. That was many years ago. I think I am finally recovered from the pain endured on the practice field that day.

The game tonight has ended. The Rockets are victorious. The Friday night lights, once again, are protected by the dedication, blood, sweat, and tears of young men that are just trying to make their dreams come true.

I make my way out of the stadium. The lights still burning brightly in the night. My thoughts are drawn to how I am not part of it anymore and as I open the car door to get in and head home, I can't stop thinking about a picture of me in that Christmas green football jersey.

I smile, and I am thankful for the memories of the dreams of young boys that wanted to play football for the honor of their hometown.

My thoughts then drift off and I wonder whatever happened to Earl Kashmere.

23

LESSON LEARNED

*I*t was a Thursday afternoon and I was stuck right in the middle of art class. That's right… I said art class. I finally admit publicly that I took art in high school.

Don't judge me.

I remember this so clearly is because I remember the music playing in class. Mrs. Cherry was young and made art fun. More importantly, she played music in her class. This day we were listening to "Wings Over America" by Paul McCartney and Wings.

Now… I would love to tell you that I was a good artist. I would also love to tell you that I was taking the class to become a better artist. Unfortunately, neither one of those reasons would be true. I took the art class for the same reasons that motivate almost every other 16-year-old male to do anything in high school… it was an easy "A" and for the girls.

It really came down to simple logic.

In 1977, I was 5'4" and 105 lbs.

Football was not an option. So, I ran cross country. Obviously, that was not going to help my reputation with the ladies. I then took choir, in the hope that I could somehow sing my way into the heart of a pretty girl (and the easy "A"). Those of you that have ever sat next to me when I sing know the unfortunate ending to my choir endeavor. Then I remembered that way back in the fifth grade I had won first place at the Ottawa County Fair for a pencil drawing.

"That's it!!!" I told myself as I scheduled my classes that year.

I would take art. How hard could it be? It was an easy "A", you get to draw, listen to music and, of course, there would be girls in the class. Girls like art, don't they?

The start of that semester went alright. Every afternoon I got to draw, paint, do calligraphy and most of all, listen to music and try to impress the ladies. However, something changed drastically one day. Instead of walking into class looking at a blank sheet of paper, there was a lump of clay on my desk. Apart from playing with Play-Doh when I was a kid, about the only thing I had ever remotely done with clay was when my buddies and I made mud balls and threw them at each other.

This was something new and I thought to myself, "I could really get into this. This might be something I may really be good at."

The ideas were just flowing and my creative juices were at an all-time high. The possibilities were endless. The concept is very simple. Take a lump of clay and shape it and mold it into something beautiful. Maybe a perfectly shaped vase or cup, maybe even something abstract that would be cool to have on my bookshelf at home.

Mrs. Cherry was up in front of the class giving instructions, but I did not have time for that. This was what I was waiting for. This would be my opportunity to do something great, something that just came naturally to me.

So, I did what I could. I took that clay and rolled it out on my desk. Visions of my finished project were so clear to me and I made a great masterpiece with the clay that day. Surely, Mrs. Cherry would be impressed by my perfect clay sculpture sitting on my desk.

I was really proud.

It had taken all of 45 seconds to create it.

There it was... the perfect ashtray.

Now the interesting thing is that I have never smoked, more importantly, no one in my family smoked. Why an ashtray? I don't have a clue. But when you think about it, this class is an easy "A" and taking any more time than that to make something else would interrupt my time listening to music and trying to impress the girls in the class.

I sat at my desk just admiring my handiwork.

"You know, this pottery stuff is easy and I am good at it," I thought to myself.

I finally found something that I was good at. With my perfect ashtray sitting on the corner of my desk, I looked around the room and took pride in the fact that I was the first one done. What could possibly be taking the other students so long? They were working and kneading the clay with their hands. Picking it up and slamming it down on the desk. I mean they were really working the clay, pressing down and working their hands into the clay. It really took them a long time to make their creations. I was just about to tell them they were doing it wrong when Mrs. Cherry told us to take our work and place it in the closet. We were going to let them dry and harden overnight and then glaze and fire them the next day.

I hurried to class on Friday. I could not wait until I would get to my perfect ashtray and start the process of glazing it and then firing it to get the finished product. I had picked out the perfect glaze for my ashtray. Black Metallic. It would be so cool when it was done. I put an extra heavy coat of the glaze on my wonderful piece of art. Something this perfect needed a little something extra and that did the trick. As I walked with my creation towards the kiln for it to be fired, Mrs. Cherry reminded us that our final grade depended on the outcome of the firing process.

I stopped in my tracks. "What did she just say?" flashed through my mind.

She continued, "Remember from class yesterday when I said that any imperfection in the clay-like air bubbles, small pieces of dirt or too much glaze would cause the clay to crack and be destroyed in the firing process."

What? I hadn't heard that!!! I looked down at my project and thought that something that looked this good could not possibly be "marred" by invisible imperfections. I placed my handiwork in the kiln confident that all would be fine.

On Monday, I walked into class with the full expectation that my little creation would be done. I walked over to the kiln and watched as other students pulled their projects from the oven. I was just about ready to look down into the kiln when Mrs. Cherry said, "Don't bother."

I looked up and she was holding scraps of what was once my perfect ashtray. It had indeed exploded in the firing process. My project was a complete failure. She started to explain to me that I had not properly worked the clay. My lump of clay was filled with tiny air bubbles that needed to be worked out the clay. That is done by slamming the clay down on the desk and forcing the air out of the clay. Also, I needed to spend time working the clay with my hands to ensure that all small pieces of dirt or stones would be worked out of the clay. If any of these imperfections were hidden in the clay it would not survive the firing process.

My project was now "Exhibit A" for the rest of the class. Instead of gaining attention because of my beautiful masterpiece, I was now the center of attention for what not to do. Mrs. Cherry told me she wanted to speak to me after class and I did not have a choice but to face the lecture that was waiting for me.

I had my response all planned out and I reluctantly stayed in my seat as class was dismissed for that day. Mrs. Cherry walked over to my table and pulled up a chair and sat silently for a few moments. I started to talk and give an excuse as to why the project failed. I was trying to blame everyone and everything. I gave every excuse in the book. I continued to tell her that I wanted another chance, but before I could finish, she held up her hand indicating that she wanted me to stop talking.

She looked up at me and said, "David, I am not concerned about your project being destroyed and that you failed. What I am concerned about is that you will miss the biggest lesson you could learn from this experience."

She continued, "David, we are all going to fail in this life. It happens. It is a part of life. However, there are reasons that you will continue to fail. Again, it's not the failure that is bad. It's the reason why you fail."

"What do you mean there are reasons why I failed?' I asked.

"You were too confident in your own plan. You did not stop to listen to the instructions. You were too busy with your own agenda and that is why you failed" she explained.

"I am not going to give you another chance to do your project. You need to learn that there are consequences for not following instructions."

I started to respond with, "It's not fair…" but she cut me off.

"David, not all things in life are fair. The sooner you understand that the better off you are going to be. In my opinion, I am being more than fair and the lesson you need to learn is not found in re-doing an ashtray in art class, but in learning to take responsibility for your actions. Once you do that, you can learn a lot by your failures."

Suddenly, I was overwhelmed with the truth of what she was saying. It wasn't the first time I had heard those words but for some reason, this time they resonated with me. I knew she was right. I was too quick to blame others for the failures in my life. Many times, I was too busy with my own agenda and missed the instructions that I needed to follow.

The result was always the same. Failure.

This took place over 40 years ago and I have shared this story with all my students when I was a teacher and I have written about it many times on my blog. I have even used this story as an illustration when I have spoken in church or in conferences.

Linda Cherry was a small-town teacher that took the time to sit down with me and help me learn a lesson that I would carry for the rest of my life. She passed away in 2010 and I am sure she never knew how much influence she would have on me.

24

RUNNER'S PANT LESS

*B*elieve it or not, the headline reads, "Runners Pant Less."
Find it... on page 120 of the 1976 Oak Harbor yearbook.

I never noticed the headline before, or if I did I must have erased it from my memory. Either way, forty-years later, there it was and the truth of it could not be more recognized than that.

I know all of us have had something that happened during our time growing up that we were embarrassed about. I have had many embarrassing things happen to me. Some of them I caused and did to myself, some not. It's a given that something is going to happen. It is inevitable. It is just what happens, and you just hope and pray it doesn't happen in front of the whole school.

I so wish I could say that.

Unfortunately... I can't.

So, what is this event and what does it have to do with that headline?

In the fall of 1975, Oak Harbor High School opened a brand-new school building. The paint in the locker room was barely dry and everything smelled fresh and clean. I showed up on the first day of practice and made my way into the locker room. I had no idea where I was supposed to be. That always seemed to be a common event for me. I never seemed to know where I was supposed to be and was always late because of it.

I walked into the locker room. The football team was already dressed, and they were heading out to start their practice. The football coach, Bill Hubans, came out of his office and looked up to see me standing there. Coach Hubans had been my 8th-grade basketball coach and he knew me.

"Lee… you're late!!! Grab a locker, get dressed and get out there with the team!" he yelled.

I didn't know how to respond. I didn't want to look him in the eye and tell him I wasn't there to join the football team. I sheepishly said, "Yes Sir." opened a locker and started to quickly get dressed. Coach Hubans went out the side door and off to coach the football team.

I sat there and stopped getting dressed. I knew I wasn't there to play football. I would love to tell a story of gridiron glory and of game-winning touchdowns, but those would forever remain locked in the dreams I would have at night. As I have documented, my football career at Oak Harbor was short lived. The hit I took from Earl Kashmere was still fresh in my memory and I simply wasn't ever going to be big enough to play the game.

For once, I was early. The new cross-country coach, Wayne Huffman, came into the locker room after a few minutes of me sitting there in front of a football locker. I did not know Coach Huffman. He was new to the Oak Harbor school system and I must have made a good impression on him because I was the first one there and I was the first runner he would introduce himself to.

He told me that the cross-country lockers were on the other side of the locker room and that he had heard I was a pretty good runner. He went on to say that someone told him there were some freshmen that would be a big part of the team and I was one of them. I was shocked that he knew who I was and that he felt I would be a big part of the team. For the first time in my life, I felt like I was recognized for who I was. I wasn't referenced as Linda Lee's little brother or the brother of the boy who was killed in that horrible train accident. I moved to the small narrow lockers that were assigned to the cross-country team and finished getting dressed.

The rest of the team showed up, got changed into their running clothes and we gathered at the back of the school to start practice. I was under the impression that we would practice there at the high school, but I was wrong. We would be practicing at Veteran's Park on the other side of town. That was my introduction to the cross-country team. We would warm-up by running the two miles to the park, only then to start practice once we got there.

The route we ran to the park would start in the back-parking lot of the high school. We would run down a path that led to Walnut Street then run a few blocks to where we would run past the front of what was now the junior high. We would head up Church Street, turn left onto Ottawa Street, go past R.C. Waters Elementary and then to Main Street where we would reach the park. That path is important to the rest of this story.

At first, we would run in a large group, all masked in the guise of team building. We had an experienced team with four or five seniors returning from the previous year. The rest of the team was made up of a few juniors and five freshmen. There were no sophomores on the team. I was a pretty good runner and made the Varsity squad. I worked and ran as hard as I could to keep that position on the team.

As soon we got into a routine of running to the park, we stopped running there together as a team. We would hurry, get dressed and take off running for the park. Usually, you would just hook up with another runner and work your way there.

After a few weeks, I started to notice something going on with the upperclassmen runners. Only the seniors would run together in a group. I started to hear stories about "hazing." For those of you that need reminding, the act of hazing is where someone or a group of people play unpleasant tricks on someone or forcing someone to do unpleasant things as part of an initiation or a rite of passage. I was hearing rumors that the seniors were grabbing the other freshman runners and hazing them. I even heard a rumor that they were planning on de-pantsing one of us. I thought that was just a joke. There wasn't a lot of talk about it and I would just hurry, get changed and start off to the park before anyone else so I could stay out in front of them.

For the most part, I got along with the seniors. My sister was a senior and I think they initially left me alone for that reason. My sister was a cheerleader and very popular. I don't think they wanted to deal with her or her boyfriend if they did something to her little brother.

That only lasted a few weeks when, as I started to leave the locker room to run to practice, one of the seniors said he needed to talk to me. I could tell something was up and I knew that he was trying to hold me up from leaving them. He was asking me a bunch of stupid questions and I finally just said that I needed to leave, and I took off running for the park.

Now they say hindsight is 20-20, I agree with that, because had I known what would happen to me, I would have stayed in the safer confines of the back-parking lot of the high school. But, I took off for the park and down the usual route that we would always run. Suddenly I heard the other seniors running after me and they were yelling, "Let's get him!!!" I kicked my running into high gear and while I wasn't exactly sure what they were going to do with me after they caught me, I was running as fast as I could run so I would not have to find out.

Running down Walnut Street, I took a quick glance behind me and noticed that, up to that point, I was keeping them away and they weren't gaining ground on me. I reached the railroad tracks and as I crossed over I saw the junior high. The thought occurred to me that if I could reach the junior high without getting caught, I could find a teacher or someone who would help me and keep them from doing whatever they were going to do to me.

I reached the bus garage and continued to sprint towards the front of the school. I rounded the corner of the front of the school and I slowed down. Classes had just ended for the day and there were kids everywhere. Not only had school let out, but all the busses filled with students from the high school were lined up all along the front of the school to pick up the junior high students that rode the bus.

Slowing down, I was sure that a teacher would intervene. The group of seniors caught me and started to tackle me. I could feel them grabbing at the bottom of my sweatpants and I suddenly realized that they were intent on de-pantsing me right then and there.

I am not sure if it was just the adrenaline or what, but I was able to fight them off and I got back up and started to run again. I was running as fast as I could, zig-zagging and dodging all the other kids as I was trying to make my way away from the school. The seniors were closing in and they caught me again. This time, right on the corner of Park and Church Street.

I couldn't fight them off this time and they managed to pull my sweatpants all the way off and were grabbing at the waistband of my running shorts. This is when time started to slow down. It was like watching a movie in slow-motion. I couldn't stop it from happening and all I could do was think, "Where are all the teachers?" hoping that someone would help me, but no one stopped them. I held on to my shorts with a death grip for as long as I could.

They simply over-powered me.

Once they pried my hands from my running shorts, I immediately grabbed the bottom of my sweatshirt and pulled it down to cover anything that might get exposed. Then suddenly they took off.

I was lying there, stunned and trying to process the fact that this took place and I wasn't dreaming. I stand up and with a firm grip of one hand on the bottom of my sweatshirt, pulling it down to cover myself up, I reach down and pull up my shorts that were wrapped around my ankles. I am safely covered back up.

There wasn't any noise. It just seemed to me there was complete silence and it is then I notice nearly every student that was moving towards their respective busses had stopped and were now staring. I look up and see high school students, classmates and kids I have known my entire life just peering out the school bus windows. Their eyes opened wide and filled with the horror of what they just witnessed.

Sure... there were some laughing and thought it was hilarious. I am also sure some were genuinely upset at what had taken place in front of them. But make no mistake, all of them were so thankful it wasn't them being humiliated in front of their friends and classmates.

I didn't know what to do, so I just grabbed my sweatpants and took off running towards the park. I got to practice, and never said a word to Coach Huffman. Other than a few comments and jokes the seniors said under their breath, it was just another day. Practice went on as normal. Right or wrong, in that era, hazing was expected. You kept your mouth shut and you moved on. Nothing else would happen to me. My initiation was now complete.

I walked home that night after practice and went straight to my bedroom. I was embarrassed and upset. I was sure that my sister had heard what happened and would have reported it to my mom. But if my sister knew, she never said a word to me or to my mother about it. I just could not help but think about who saw what and how humiliating it was. I didn't sleep much. I could only think about what I was going to face the next day at school.

I wasn't wrong. The next day, all hell broke loose.

The first indication was when I had a friend of mine come up to me as I walked into the school. The first thing out of his mouth was, "Hey, nudie!!" I just stopped in my tracks. The only thing I wanted to do was to turn around and head back home. Unfortunately, I knew that wasn't an option.

I continued to walk down the hall towards my locker. No one else said a word to me. They either hadn't heard of the event or were just being told as I walked down the hall. Either way, by the time they took homeroom attendance, I could tell most people had heard.

As I sat down in my homeroom class, I had a few people ask me what happened, and I told them. They said that my version isn't what really happened and that I was lying. Can you believe that? Why would I lie? I was there, and shouldn't I know what happened? One version they heard was that I was completely naked running across the whole front of the junior high and that I had done it intentionally. I was streaking and took my own clothes off. Then, after I was caught by a teacher in the front of the school, I blamed the seniors. Another version had it that I was crying like a baby and ran home completely naked to my mommy. At least in the second version, they were correct in that it was the seniors that de-pantsed me. However, the details of both versions were not even close to the truth of the event.

Isn't it funny how fast a story can spread throughout the student body? I could sense their eyes peering at me and I could only imagine the versions that were being told. Like most things, a story gets twisted and sometimes the facts are not part of the story that is being told. By the time I left the homeroom, to head to my first-period class, I had already heard enough to know that this whole event was not going to end well.

I never made it to my first-period class. As I walked out the door of my homeroom, the assistant principal, Mr. Johns, was waiting for me outside the door. He told me I needed to head to the main school office. On my way there, I had to walk by the senior hallway and all eyes were looking at me. For some reason, I felt like I was in trouble for something. I didn't ask for this and I tried to avoid it at all costs. Maybe I should have let them catch me in the parking lot in the back of the high school. I still would have been de-pantsed, but no one would be any wiser about it and it would just be a rumor that would run its course and disappear in a few days. But this wasn't going to work out that way.

I walked into the office and I was quickly led into Mr. Johns' office. There sat Larry St Clair, a police officer with the Oak Harbor Police Department. Larry asked me for details and I told him. He told me that there was a complaint filed with the police department and that he needed to find out the facts. He already heard a bunch of different versions. I told him that my version was the real story and he wrote down everything I said. Then he asked for the specific names of the students that did this. I told him that I didn't want to say. Larry said that he already knew but he needed confirmation from me. I was put in a difficult position and after about 10 minutes of pressure from Mr. Johns and Officer St Clair, I finally told them the names of the seniors that did it. I was then taken out of the office and was told to sit in a chair in the office hallway just down from Mr. Johns' office.

What happened next was a never-ending parade of people moving in and out of the office. Coach Huffman was taken in and out the office, then all the seniors, each of them glaring at me as they walked out of the office. Soon after, I saw the parents of the seniors each brought in and out of the office with their sons. At times, the discussions in that office would get loud and I was sure there was shouting.

I sat out in the hallway for a few hours. I couldn't hear any of the conversations. The only thing I was aware of was the glare from each senior as they left the office with their parent. I was told to head to class and no one from the administration of Oak Harbor High

School ever said another word to me about the incident.

Later that day, I would find out through the "rumor mill" that the seniors who participated in the act were kicked off the team. The other rumor was that the only reason they were kicked off the team was that my mom was the one who filed a police report and had threatened a lawsuit. Truth was, up to that point, my mom had no idea that it even took place.

I wanted to have things just go back to normal. But I guess that was too much to hope for. A strange silence hovered wherever I went that day. It was like the other students were told not to speak of it to me directly. I am sure that it was being talked about but none of the conversation was with me. By the time I went to practice that day, the lockers of those involved were cleaned out. We didn't practice at the park anymore and we would run at the school for the remainder of the season.

I ran on the varsity squad before the incident and I ran on it afterward. I would continue to run the last few meets and participate in the league championships at the end of the year. After the season, I was awarded my Varsity Letter. Jim Blausey and I were the first in our class to letter. I deserved that letter. I earned it. I worked hard for it. I would have lettered anyway. People said I would not have received it if I hadn't cried to my mom and told on the seniors. Now that never made any sense to me. I did not cry to my mom. I wasn't the one who told her. As a matter of fact, I have no idea how she found out. I've never had a discussion with her about the event.

As far as getting the seniors kicked off the team, I was forced to give the names of those that did it. The yearbook says that one of them said that the discipline they received was unfair. The only one who was treated unfairly was me. I never received an apology from any of the seniors. In a strange twist, I somehow was blamed for them getting kicked off the team. In today's world, there would have been a lawsuit against the school by all parties involved.

I have to say that I changed because of this incident. It was the beginning of a quest that I made for myself. I was already tired of only being known as Linda Lee's little brother or the brother of those boys who were killed at the end of Benton Street. Now I was known as the person who was de-pantsed in front of the high school student body and the person who got all the seniors kicked off the cross-country team. I tried to hide my frustration and I tried to be above it, but the damage had been done and I had to find something that was mine. I had to find a place where I wasn't someone's little brother or the kid that got de-pantsed in front of the whole school.

There was nothing I could do. I was a freshman and it would be another year or so before I could drive and transfer to someplace where I could start over. I felt as if I was on my own. I had to deal with it by myself. So, I did my time and after I received my driver's license after my sophomore year, I made the decision to transfer. I left the Oak Harbor school system and made a new start somewhere else. I got a full-time job at H.J. Heinz and worked from 11:00 PM to 7:00 AM every night and went to school during the day (something that is not legal today). I paid for my own tuition to attend a private, Christian school for my junior and senior years of school.

I don't regret the decision, it was what was best for me at the time. I tried to hide it and I never told anyone the real reason why I left Oak Harbor High School. But I must admit, to this very day, I feel like I was cheated out of graduating from the hometown I grew up in. That is part of the underlying motivation for this book. It is an attempt to re-connect with the footsteps I put down all those years ago. There are not many things in life I would want to change. I am who I am because of these stories about my life. The good and the bad. However, if there was one story that I wish I could change, it would be this one.

Whenever someone asks me where I went to high school, I still tell them proudly, Oak Harbor.

I know it isn't the truth and I know you won't find my senior picture in the 1979 Harbor Lites yearbook. The truth is, that picture faded into anonymity on an October afternoon in 1975 on the corner of Park and Church Street, when a hazing, a believed harmless prank, ended up not being so harmless.

25

ONLY THE PORCH LIGHTS REMAIN THE SAME

*T*he Ottawa County Fair … the sunbaked, annual, end-of-summer celebration of food, music, rides, farm animals and carny games. It was an aimless, all-day, all-evening event of wandering around the fairgrounds. It always seemed to me to be the biggest, longest party of the summer.

Held for a week on the sprawling fairgrounds located between Oak Harbor and Port Clinton, it was the last blast of summer. The last of the good times before the unforgiving timetable of the real world kicked in before fall.

Soon the whistles of the football coaches would signal the end of summer and a gentle reminder that school was just around the corner. But for now, the week was filled with life-long memories of being a kid in the middle of the county at the end of another summer. No matter how old you were or how many times you had been there before, you were always a kid at the fair.

The 4-H kids, in addition to the farm families, would all be present having driven in from the corners of the county to display their projects. Their prize livestock and finest crops were in the competition for bragging rights. People would arrive for the nighttime concerts in front of the grandstand; there would be harness racing, live radio broadcasts and when you were young, non-stop flirting with people you'd never seen before and probably would never see again.

Sure, it was corny. You weren't supposed to take it too seriously. It was all supposed to be fun and maybe a wink to the past. Maybe it was to be taken with a grain of salt so that you could escape for a few days from what was really going on around the world. Nothing that took place during those few days of the summer was ever meant to be permanent except for good memories forever ingrained into our conscience.

Nothing extraordinary about any of it. Except for everything.

As a young child, the highlight of each summer was marked by the annual county fair. For several days in July, kiddie rides, games of chance, concession stands and fun houses were erected in the heart of our county. When I was really young, unlike some of my friends who would go to the fair every day, I was usually only able to get to the fair one day during that week. I looked forward to it for months. I look back at the time now and realize that my anticipation for the event was much more exciting than the real thing. When my day finally came around, I spent the day shoving cotton candy in my mouth, riding the giant swing ride over and over and going to look at all the animals.

At the end of the day, I'd crawl sleepy-eyed into the backseat clutching cheap trinkets won playing everyone is a "winner" carnival games. It was the highlight of my summer.

As my summers accumulated and I advanced towards junior high, summer life became all about friends. My small group of friends and I rode our bikes all over town on long summer days creating our own adventures to shake up this small-town life. Life was filled with little league baseball, Teagarden's pool and most importantly... the fair. These were the most important aspects of our summers. However, there was an underlying strange realization, we were just starting to discover but not ready to admit just yet, that girls weren't so yucky after all.

Summer still ended with the fair. But instead of playing games and riding rides, the focus had shifted. We now walked around the fair. We walked in packs. We were all just walking around trying to look cool.

We weren't.

However, there was strength in numbers. Even though not one of us would ever admit to it, our pack walked around hoping to run into the group of junior high girls that were gathered safely in their own pack. We would walk until we grew tired. Tired of daring each other to do outlandish acts. Tired of acting like little immature kids. Tired of trying to act like we were older than we were.

The truth was... we really wanted to go ride the rides like we did when we were little.

But here we were suspended somewhere between childhood and being a teenager. It was all wrapped up in the security of living in a place and time where time seemed to stand still. All the people and all the houses that surrounded you were as familiar as the things in your own room. You believed it would always stay the same.

The dreams of life beyond the town limits of Oak Harbor were still off in the distance. But as much as we believed, something deep inside of us knew the truth. Slowly, change was happening. Soon enough, little league baseball would end and we would be made to face the reality that only a few of my friends would continue to play baseball in high school.

I wasn't one of them.

I suddenly had the overwhelming feeling that I walked out of my childhood and into the next phase of my life. I wasn't ready. I wanted to stay there in the comfort of the summer nights of Oak Harbor. But I knew I couldn't. I was now fourteen. I slept under a roof that belonged to someone else and in a bed my father bought. Nothing was mine, except my fears and the growing knowledge that not every road was going to lead home anymore.

Things were changing. I would hear some of my own friends start to talk about making plans on leaving the safety of our hometown. I started to hear the other side of growing up in Oak Harbor. The negative. In my mind, the place was perfect, almost sacred.

Looking back, I know it wasn't perfect and obviously not sacred. It was clear that my feelings were found in a place that was caught up in the reluctance to move from the 1950's to the 1970's.

Before I knew it, I found myself in high school.

Going to the fair was now focused on running into other kids from school and seeing who had coupled up or broken up over the last few months, triumphs or casualties of summer.

We no longer walked in packs. I would usually just hang out with Bryan. It kept the competition down and I would not have to be embarrassed by that one friend that always acted like an idiot.

During fair week, when the sun went down, that magical familiar feeling of youth slipped over me once again. Those exciting feelings of not knowing what would happen next would overwhelm me. I could not help but think that there was the possibility that the crush you had might see you and smile at you.

When it looked like no one was around, I worked up the courage to go on the Kamikaze, a ride that shuttled you in giant, nauseating upside-down loops. I screamed at the top of my lungs while "Do Ya" by the Electric Light Orchestra blasted through the ride's crappy speakers, and I felt like a badass.

I wasn't.

At the time, there was no greater disappointment than when the fair packed up and left town with all your wishes still unfulfilled.

That last night at the fair, in the darkness of night, Bryan and I walked home from the fairgrounds. Our ride left us, and we had no choice but to walk the four miles back to Oak Harbor. At sixteen, the premise of walking home on a hot summer night seemed to be perfectly logical. It was so dark that it seemed you couldn't see past your next step. The only light coming from the moon.

We took our time. There was no need to hurry. It didn't seem like there was that much to go back to.

Bryan and I talked about everything on that long walk home. We talked about our childhood, our families. We talked about music, what we liked and disliked. We talked about girls. We talked about our future. He told me what his plans were for his life. Bryan wanted to leave the tiny confines of Oak Harbor, Ohio, as soon as he could. He wanted to see the world and the sooner the better.

For me, I wasn't exactly panicking about my plans. I don't think

up to that point in my life I had ever given a second thought about
what I was going to do with my future. I was just sixteen years old.
To me, the future was for someone else to worry about.

Then the subject matter changed. We started to talk about what
we believed in. Bryan was asking all kind of questions. That was odd
for Bryan because there were topics he just would not discuss. But
not this night…we talked about everything. Bryan knew me as well as
anyone can know another person. We were as close as brothers. He
knew I went to church, and there were even times he went with me.
He never gave any impression that he was interested in learning more
about it and he never asked me any questions about it. He knew that
my faith was very important to me, but I never once considered
sharing my faith and what I really believed to anyone before,
especially him. After all, he knew my weaknesses and my failures as
well as anyone.

But on this night, this dark ridiculous night, he asked and I shared
my faith and told him what I believed. Maybe my boldness came
from the fact that it was pitch black and I could not see his reaction
to my words, or maybe because Bryan couldn't see my hands shaking
in fear, but for whatever reason, I said it out loud. Bryan never said a
word in argument. He just kept asking questions and I tried to
answer them as best I could. Soon our conversation drifted to
another subject and nothing more was discussed about our faith.

We had walked almost all the way to town when suddenly Bryan
and I stopped talking. It seemed as if there was nothing left to say. I
wanted to stay there, in that night, but I knew I couldn't.

Things were about to change again.

Walking through that neighborhood I grew up in, I realized that
there was a time I knew every family on the block, their kid's names
and the names of their dogs. But most of those families were gone
now. The ones who stayed were not the same. The world was
moving on.

Eventually, I made my way home and walking past each one of
those homes, I started to realize something. I was beginning to
understand that in each home, with its Ford parked out front, white
bread on the table and TV set glowing blue in the falling night, there
were people with stories. There were families bound together in the

pain and the struggle to make it in life. I was just starting out on my journey to figure out what life was about. Growing up in Oak Harbor, protected by the outside world, I wasn't even sure I knew what "real" life was anymore, but I knew I had a lot to learn and my quest to finally find it was a long way off.

Walking up to my driveway, I noticed what a beautiful night it was - lit by the moon. The world smelled fresh and clean. I turned the handle of the front door and opened it. Like always, there was my mom sitting at the kitchen table reading the newspaper. As I walked into the room, she put her paper down and stood up. She gave me a big hug. She never said a word and neither did I. We didn't have to, for in that moment I felt like a kid again. Life and all its responsibilities were knocking on the door, but for tonight, they would have to wait.

I never went to the fair again.

Bryan and I didn't really accomplish anything that night. At least that is what I thought at the time. There would be other nights that summer where we would hang out and try to be cool. We always failed. But the sad truth is there wasn't ever another night just like that one.

Our brotherhood was forever etched in stone and would never end, but when that summer ended the remaining high school years that lay ahead would find Bryan and I moving in different directions.

Once school started we never hung out again, at least not like we did before. The last time was that last night at the fair. That night and the long walk home will always be set apart in my memory and in my heart.

Everything changed that night and only the porch lights remained the same.

26

I NEVER HAD A CHANCE

I got my driver's license when I turned 16. It was the first time I felt like I was part of the world and not bound by the unforgiving signs of our town limits.

I felt untethered, independent and unrestricted.

It makes me grin when I think about it now because I was still bound by the town limit signs. I just changed my mode of transportation. I went from a 10-speed bicycle to a Ford Pinto which only really meant I could drive the loop around town a little faster. Not much faster, mind you, but just enough to make me feel free. I would drive my car in the same continuous, languorous, tedious, life-sucking regular loop around town.

A typical summer night would be as follows: I would pull out of my driveway on Locust Street and drive south to the stoplight by Denny's Gulf Station. Then I would make a left turn onto Water Street and drive slowly to see if any of my friends were at Van Atta's Dairy Queen. If no one was there, I would continue down the street and turn left onto Finke Road and drive through Veteran's Park to see if there were any softball or baseball games going on. If there were any girls playing tennis on the courts next to the road, that was an extra bonus.

In today's world, I would have been handcuffed, interrogated and probably body-searched over why I was sitting at the park watching ball games and girls playing tennis from the front seat of my car. But not back then. I can't tell you how many times I sat there parked in my car, watching from the front seat, trying to look and be cool. I wanted to talk to the cute girls playing tennis or to the other girls that were just walking around the park trying to look as cool as I was trying to be.

I sat there trying to get enough nerve to start conversations with girls whose names I knew and went to school with since kindergarten. I could never pull the trigger. I would just swallow my confidence and promise myself that tomorrow night would be different.

"I will do it for sure tomorrow" I would say to myself, as the music blared from FM 104.7 on my stereo.

I would sit there alone hoping that the station would at least play "Cold as Ice" by Foreigner or "Do You Feel Like We Do" by Peter Frampton when those girls would walk by, so I could turn it up even louder and they would "hear" that I was cool.

Thinking about it now… sitting in my car like that was probably weird. I just never considered that possibility when I was doing it.

Eventually, I would grow tired of just sitting there in my car with the music blaring from my Kenwood Stereo system that cost more than the car I was driving. It never dawned on me at the time, but when I would pull up in my dark blue rusted out Pinto, I was parking next to the never-ending sea of Camaro's and Trans Am's that always seemed to be owned by every "cool kid" in Oak Harbor.

I was lying to myself. I would tell myself again that tomorrow night would be different.

Deep down, I knew, I never had a chance.

On nights that the park was empty, I would then just cruise the loop around town. I would make the left turn onto Main Street and drive down to Locust Street and make the only right turn I would take for the next hour or so. Once on Locust Street, I would turn left onto South Railroad Street then turn left onto Benton Street, drive to Howard and Vern's, turn left onto Water Street and drive through the main portion of the town, all two blocks of it. Finally, I would come back to the intersection where Denny's Gulf Station was and turn left back onto Locust Street and the loop was complete. If you drove the speed limit, it took about 8 minutes to complete the whole loop.

So, there I'd be in my Pinto, stereo blasting, just hoping and waiting for my favorite song to play one more time on the radio before I called it a night. Sometimes my friends would be with me and we would inch ever closer to driving past those town limit signs. But sure enough, we would make the left turn onto the loop, none of us really talking about anything as we drove around. We were listening to the radio and filling our heads with ideas of what life would be for us and what was going to happen to us in the future. We were daydreaming of life on the outside, while keeping our eyes peeled on the familiar sights that we have passed thousands of times before as if we were going to see something we hadn't seen already.

As I pulled up to the stoplight at the corner of Church Street and Water Street, I would slowly drive through the main stretch of town. I would pass the once majestic armory.

It now sat old, abandoned, empty.

Its purpose now was just a place where bored teens would hang out. The front steps of the armory were inviting and friendly to those who needed a place to feel normal with their friends.

Make no mistake, there is and was different groups of kids that made up the teen population of our small town.

The group that usually hung out on the steps of the armory were those kids that didn't fit in the molds that other teens fit in. They usually weren't the band kids or the athletes. They definitely were not the cool kids, but rather the kids that were smokers and were often called "hoods" or "burnouts."

In today's world, the term hood is different than it was back then. Today it is an urban term that acknowledges someone from a certain neighborhood. But back then, the term "hood" was a derivative of "hoodlum," which indicated a person who was always causing trouble. The term "burnout" was given because most people were convinced that all of them were "high" and burned out on drugs.

Most of them grew their hair long and wore jean jackets or an old army coat. There were rules when it came to their jacket: They

NEVER let anyone else wear it. It wasn't a letterman's jacket, but it was just as important. They never washed it. They wore it in school, in the house, and over their Led Zeppelin or Aerosmith t-shirt.

They never took it off.

In reflection, the term "burnout" wasn't the kind of designation they willingly chose. It was a name given to them, a label they inherited. It's a cruel tag for anyone—but especially for a kid. Burnouts came from working-class families and even if it wasn't true, most people believed they were only enrolled in vocational classes at school because they weren't smart enough or good enough to make it in "regular" school. Nothing was further from the truth.

The truth was they were regular, smart, athletic, good kids that, even in our small town, were pushed to the outskirts of life because they didn't fit in. They were evaluated by their last name and where they lived and where they sat in the cafeteria at lunch. They were judged by things they could not control or change. They rebelled by defiantly smoking Marlboro Reds in public places like the front steps of the armory and having a non-conforming attitude towards the social norms of what and who they were expected to be.

Personally... I envied them. They had found a family, a community if you will, where they could be themselves and not what someone else wanted them to be. I always believed that this group of "hoods" and "burnouts" were always trying to hold on to something they didn't want to lose. But as I look back, I now believe that they were just trying to let go of social status.

While I was not a "member" of that group, I admit there were times that I took comfort in hanging out on the steps of the armory with some of them. After I endured the de-pantsing incident, I was more of a loner than ever before. In addition, I was struggling with what my faith was telling me how I should live while trying to fit in with kids I had grown up with. I wasn't a strong enough Christian to stand up for my faith and I made choices and did things that even to this day I am embarrassed to have allowed myself to be a part of.

I know I cannot change those decisions all those years ago, but I still regret that I wasn't a good witness of my faith and my relationship with Jesus Christ. For so many years, I would be there at church on Sunday mornings and Wednesday nights, then go into hiding when I was with my friends in Oak Harbor. I never said a word to anyone about my faith. Even after I left Oak Harbor High School and enrolled in a Christian school in Fremont, I still struggled with being a good example of a believer. I excelled at being an undercover agent (in hiding) when it came to my faith. I was good at hiding my faith from my friends and I was just as good at hiding the things I shouldn't have been doing from my mother.

I was a square peg trying to fit in the round holes of acceptance.

I did not fit anywhere.

The kids that hung out at the armory were always the nicest and accepting people. They allowed me to come and go as I pleased, but I wasn't a real member of that group.

I would drive my car by them as they congregated there, and they knew that if they needed a ride I was someone who would pick them up and take them where they needed to go.

Sometimes, we would drive around the same loop I'd driven all night.

As that summer wore on, driving around the loop would start to feel different. I never told anyone that I was leaving Oak Harbor High School and that I would soon be starting school in Fremont for my junior and senior years.

The armory was still there for now, but I knew it was ending and changing for me. I did not know what would become of some of the best friendships I had created by driving that old rusted Pinto around the loop.

The people I knew were going in one direction and I was going in another.

During the last few days of summer the radio blasted all the way through my loops around Oak Harbor and I couldn't talk to anyone. I was consumed with one thought and as much as I wanted it to have a different outcome, I knew I never had a chance.

27

AN ORDINARY, AVERAGE GUY

There were so many things I wanted to be as I grew up in Oak Harbor.

Some of these career choices are funny to me now that I look back on them.

A pilot, a singer, a musician, a barber (this is the first public admission that I thought about becoming a barber), a baseball player, a football player, a great speaker, a great writer and a great teacher are just a "few of the things" I wanted to be growing up.

When I was a kid, the thing I wished for most was to be talented. No, not just talented. I wanted to be special. I wanted to stand out from the crowd. I wanted to change the world with something I could do. I wanted to be someone. I wanted to be different and rise above average and be great at something. I wanted my hometown of Oak Harbor, Ohio, to remember who I was and I wanted my family to be proud of me. The problem was I wasn't great at anything.

Not one thing.

I remember always thinking… "If only I had enough talent."

Like most boys growing up, I dreamt of being a professional athlete. Playing a sport I loved and getting paid for it was just the ticket for the dreams of a young skinny kid from Oak Harbor, Ohio.

If I only had enough talent.

When you are 5'4" as a sophomore and weigh a solid 85 lbs. dressed in your football uniform with full pads and helmet... it was painfully obvious that football was not going to be in my future. The fact that I grew 9 inches during the summer between my 10th and 11th-grade years did not make the prospect of being a professional athlete any clearer. Yes, I was 6' 2", but I also only weighed 130 lbs. A strong wind could and would knock me over.

While, I was not the worst player on any of the teams I played on, the evidence was clear that I was not going to take Hank Aaron's place in the Major Leagues, nor was I going to play for the Cleveland Browns at any time in my life.

If I only had enough talent.

I had always thought of myself as artistic. Why I thought that I do not have a clue. I have always loved to draw and be creative. I tried to be artistic and there was a time I thought I was pretty good at it. Maybe I thought that because when I was in the fifth grade I won a first-place ribbon at the Ottawa County Fair for a pencil drawing. I guess it gave me enough confidence to convince myself that I was talented. I thought this way until I compared my ability to those around me when I took art classes at Oak Harbor High School. The lessons learned in Mrs. Cherry's art class made me suddenly realize that my artistic ability was somewhat to be desired. In other words, not so good.

If only I had enough talent.

Then there was the period in my life when I dreamed of what it would be like to be the lead singer of a band. I believed I could sing all the notes of my favorite songs and bands when the music was blasting through the $10.00 speakers of my 1976 Ford Pinto.

It's funny how we convince ourselves that we are as talented as our favorite singer we hear on our radio. Who of us has never sang their heart out using a hairbrush as a microphone? The sad truth is that I found out how lacking I truly was when I tried out to sing a solo for our choir concert. It was not pretty.

If I only had enough talent.

I have written numerous times about my search to find what my talent was in life and I must admit, when I reflect at my life, I am hard pressed to state exactly what my talent ever was.

I have had to come to terms with the fact that I will not be remembered, not even in the small town I was raised in. I have not changed the world and for the most part, the only true mark that I will ever make will be the slab of stone that my family puts up to mark my burial plot. I have come to accept the fact that I am just an ordinary, average guy.

I accepted long ago that the world never revolved around me. It kind of blows your mind when you first realize this. The truth is, in 50 years, no one will remember me. No one's going to care. There's something unsettling about that, but in a strange twist it is liberating as well.

When you come to terms of being ordinary, of being average, possibly even below average, the stress and anxiety of feeling inadequate dissipates. The knowledge and acceptance of your average existence will free you to accomplish what you truly wish to accomplish with no judgments and no lofty expectations.

When I accepted being ordinary and average, I grew a deep appreciation for life's experiences. I have learned to measure myself by new, healthier means: the pleasures of simple friendship, creating something with my hands, helping a person in need, reading a good book, having a good conversation with my wife and hanging out with my grandchildren.

Sounds boring, doesn't it? That's because these things are average.

Maybe they're average for a reason.

I believe they are average because they are what matters.

Life for the ordinary, average me is when my wife is happy to see me after a long day at work. It's when she texts me just to say, I love you. Life is knowing that there is no one I want to spend more time with than with my wife.

Life for the ordinary, average me is when my grandson Brody comes into the room, hugs me and yells, "Grandpa" because he is so excited to see me. It's lying on the floor, playing with NASCAR cars and going to the races with my grandson Indiana.

Life for the ordinary, average me is having my children express words of love for each other and for Pam and me.

Life for the ordinary, average me is sending stupid, ridiculous selfies to my daughter Cassidy and have her send one back to me. It is also when I hear her sing.

It's when my daughter Crystal asks me for advice and for my help.

It's when my son Nathan and I have long conversations about music and our love for the Cleveland Browns and Indians.

Life is when my son Adam and I are talking to each other in love.

Life is winning the battle so far to NOT be that old guy yelling at the local kids to stay off my lawn.

It's a sunny day in the garage, being creative and working on another project with my hands.

It's when someone likes something I wrote.

It's acknowledging my failures and coming to an understanding of my responsibilities for them.

Life is forgiving those who don't deserve it.

Life is learning to forgive yourself.

It's attending a church that I love.

Life is giving more than we take. It is trying to leave things around us just a little better than we found them.

Life for the ordinary, average me is all of this and more.

The list of what makes life special for me grows each day. I could not possibly list them all here.

Sometimes I get caught up in what I could have been. I know that haunted me for years. However, as I sojourn to the backside of my 50's, I have come to peace and acceptance that I will forever be ordinary and average.

Nothing special… just ordinary and average.

Ultimately, life is being okay with being just that.

EPILOGUE

When I reminisce about my childhood summers, I think of the smell of sun and sweat on my skin after playing outside all day long. I think of the sizzle of sparklers and the big colorful explosions of fireworks with their sulfuric scent lingering in the air on July 4th celebrations at Veterans Park.

I think of the smell of chlorine and blood-shot eyes from swimming in Teagarden's pool.

I think of cupping my small hands around fireflies and dropping them into mason jars, little pieces of summer I wish I could have treasured forever.

I can still remember the way my heart would race when I knew it was a baseball game day.

I miss the feeling of pure joy of being flanked by my best friends on our bikes. Experiencing our first taste of freedom and being able to take ourselves anywhere within the town limits, powered by the adrenaline pumping through our veins with each spin of our silver spokes.

I wish I could have bottled all those feelings all those years ago, like those fireflies in that mason jar. To once again feel that youthful freedom and the delicious possibility of how any given night might end. I'd open the lid and breathe in the smallest sample to make it last.

In closing, this has been such a wonderful experience for me. Can you imagine going back to your roots and reliving your youth? You see yourself grow up and you see yourself make mistakes. You see your heart get broken and you experience the loss of loved ones. However, you also get to relive the good things and the friendships that were such a big part of your life. That is what I have relived by writing these stories.

My hope is that some of you that took the time to read this book will come away with an appreciation of another place and time. Maybe your memories were stirred, and you can relate to my journey to once again find the footprints of your youth.

I hope that you once again feel the freedom of the last day of school that stretched across three blissful sunburnt summer months. I hope your memories will allow you to relive growing up with a deep appreciation of summer nights that can never be as good as they were when you were young, especially in the confines of your sleepy little town.

I have more stories to tell but I had to edit this down and take some out. I struggled with knowing what stories to leave in and which ones to take out. There is a fear that some of the best stories were cut from this project. Who knows? Maybe one day I will publish them.

At the end of the day, that doesn't matter.

What does matter is knowing that I was homegrown and raised in a small town in Ohio called Oak Harbor.

A place where my footprints can still be found.

PICTURES

Here are a few pictures that relate to these stories. (Upper Left) This is a picture taken in 1963 just before we moved to Oak Harbor. (Upper Right) My kindergarten picture from 1966. (Bottom Left) School picture of my brother Bobby taken just before the accident. (Bottom Right) My favorite picture of my brother.

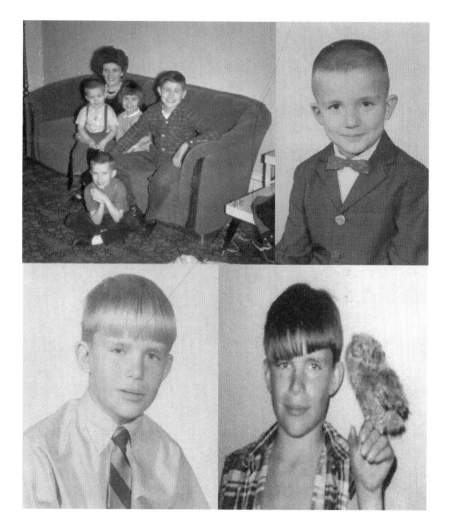

Robert Allen Lee

Larry Mills   Harold "Buster" Chandler

My mom and dad celebrating 65 years of marriage on July 22, 2017

Before the dreams of being a professional athlete were dashed upon the rocks of reality.

(Left) Heading towards the finish line in a cross-country meet in 1975. (Below Right) My first car, a Ford Pinto. The stories this car could tell as it made endless loops around town.

Bryan and I getting ready to pick up our dates for the
Homecoming Dance.

A Momma's boy.

ABOUT THE AUTHOR

David Michael Lee grew up in Oak Harbor, Ohio. He is a graduate of Liberty University and is a former high school administrator and teacher. He is the author of the blog, *"Footprints of a Legacy Left Behind."* David and his wife, Pam, are the  parents of four children and two grandchildren.

David Michael Lee

Made in the USA
Lexington, KY
17 April 2018